**Pra
DREAMS ARE YOUR**

"A splendid overview of the myriad kinds of dreams that visit all of us during sleep. . . . A very readable and practical book."
— **Calvin S. Hall,**
dream researcher and author

"An excellent book that handles the complex matter of dreams simply via short, enlightening case histories with which a reader can easily identify."
— **Arnold A. Hutschnecker, M.D.,**
author of *A Will to Live*

"*Dreams Are Your Truest Friends* is a greatly needed book. It shows with delightful simplicity how dreams are very private, intimate communications a dreamer makes to oneself."
— **Dr. Ruth P. Berkeley,**
psychiatrist and psychoanalyst

Most Berkley Books are available at special quantity discounts for bulk purchases for sales promotions, premiums, fund raising, or educational use. Special books or book excerpts can also be created to fit specific needs.

For details, write or telephone Special Markets, The Berkley Publishing Group, 200 Madison Avenue, New York, New York 10016; (212) 951-8891.

DREAMS ARE YOUR TRUEST FRIENDS

JOSEPH KATZ, PH.D.

BERKLEY BOOKS, NEW YORK

If you purchased this book without a cover, you should be aware that this book is stolen property. It was reported as "unsold and destroyed" to the publisher, and neither the author nor the publisher has received any payment for this "stripped book."

The author gratefully acknowledges permission from the following sources to reprint material in their control:

Doubleday & Company, Inc., for material from *Man & Times* by J. B. Priestley. Copyright © 1964 by Aldus Books Limited. Published by Doubleday & Company, Inc.

Harper & Row Publishers, Inc., for material from *You Can't Go Home Again* by Thomas Wolfe, copyright 1934, 1937, 1938, 1939, 1940 by Maxwell Perkins.

Readers Subscription, Inc., for material from *The Griffin*, Vol. 9, No. 8, August 1960.

The University of Chicago Press for material from *The Gilgamesh Epic and Old Testament Parallels* by A. Heidel, © 1946, 1949 University of Chicago, all rights reserved; second edition, 1949.

DREAMS ARE YOUR TRUEST FRIENDS

A Berkley Book / published by arrangement with
Simon & Schuster, Inc.

PRINTING HISTORY
Simon & Schuster edition published 1975
Berkley edition / May 1994

All rights reserved.
Copyright © 1975 by Joseph Katz.
This book may not be reproduced in whole or in part, by mimeograph or any other means, without permission.
For information address: Simon & Schuster, Inc., 630 Fifth Avenue, New York, New York 10020.

ISBN: 0-425-14142-X

BERKLEY®
Berkley Books are published by The Berkley Publishing Group,
200 Madison Avenue, New York, New York 10016.
BERKLEY and the "B" design are
trademarks of Berkley Publishing Corporation.

PRINTED IN THE UNITED STATES OF AMERICA

10 9 8 7 6 5 4 3 2 1

ACKNOWLEDGMENTS

Gratitude is due my true friends and colleagues Mildred Newman and Dr. Bernard Berkowitz, who suggested and encouraged the writing of this book. They most graciously offered their full help in every way they could.

I wish to thank Lynn Nesbit, literary agent for International Famous Agency, and especially Michael V. Korda, Editor-in-Chief of Simon and Schuster, for their expert criticism and suggestions, which were indispensable in shaping and developing this book most effectively.

I am especially indebted to all the talented dreamers of this book who so generously shared their innermost lives with everyone; also to my many students and the people I have worked with, who have added fresh directions to my feelings and thinking on dreams.

For
Estelle,
and our children,
Nina, Vivian, Bert

Contents

~~~~~~

Preface

~~~~~~

The desires and fears that people have throughout their lives appear in their dreams as an aid to understanding and coping with their many worries and pressures. In this book the special problems of women and men and how they may be faced and overcome in their dreams are presented on a broad scope. Additional chapters treat the handling of children's dreams, the turbulence of adolescent dreams, and how dreams actually work as warnings to individuals, actually serving as vital protectors of life itself. There are special chapters analyzing the dreams of scientists and explorers, writers and painters, warriors and heroes, Biblical dreams, and dreams that predict events— all designed to demonstrate the vital role of dreams throughout the ages in helping us to understand ourselves better and so lead better lives.

The Power of Dreaming

Among the legends of the Blackfoot Indians there is a tale of the early people who were poor and naked and did not know how to live. Old Man, their maker, said, "Go to sleep and get power. Whatever animals appear in your dream, pray and listen." And, the story concludes, "that was how the first people got through the world, by the power of their dreams."

The power of dreaming has not diminished over the ages. We no longer endow animals or totems with godly powers to save us; instead, we turn more and more within ourselves to find new storehouses of meaning, understanding, and power to overcome the original panic of childhood aloneness.

The essential ingredient of the good dream is that we are not alone; there is always someone behind us. The animal or child spirit within us is the true spark and driving thrust of life, and it need never leave us; the dream is a nightly reminder of the unsuspected resources of the ages residing within, waiting to be tapped.

Thus, the dreams of all ages reach for the stars: the

impossible, out of reach, forbidden, perilous, but irresistibly tempting and desirable. The wild dreams of the past have, for better or worse, that uncanny knack of becoming the reality of today. The moon is no longer out of reach.

Ours is at once a blissful and a cruel world; the roots of both reach far into the unknown depths of the dream and spring forth as the best and the worst of which we are capable. From the dream come both creation and love on the one hand, and destruction and hate on the other—the opposite uses of power. The name of the game is power, and the dream is both its source and its purveyor.

The dream can offer a vital solution to a critical problem of survival, or it can become an excuse for arrogant ambition. History, says Stephen Dedalus in Joyce's *Ulysses*, "is a nightmare from which I am trying to wake up." The nightmare has to do with the terrible price men pay for their ambitions—and especially their successes. The attainment of success and power can bring out the worst in a person; as it evokes all childhood terrors and guilts it makes one erratic and self-punitive to stave off the most dreaded consequences of finally attaining one's greatest desires.

Freud recognized the power of the dream as "the royal road to the unconscious"—that it is our basic wishes and the fears and guilts which accompany them that make the world go round. But Freud himself underestimated the essential life-saving and self-preservative function of the dream which later-day physiological research was to prove. We now know that the dream is as necessary as breathing; it is, among other things, a safety valve outlet for the inevitable buildup of anxiety resulting from the tensions of life. Dreaming also helps us to cope.

Essentially, this is the approach of Jung:

Within each of us there is another whom we do not know. He speaks to us in dreams and tells us how differently he sees us from how we see ourselves. When we find ourselves in an insolubly difficult situation, this stranger in us can sometimes show us a light which is more suited than anything else to change our attitude fundamentally, namely just that attitude which has led us into the difficult situation.

The dream is our own creation and we shape it as we see fit—either for creativity and fulfillment or to thwart, punish, or divide ourselves. The dream that reflects the divided self offers the opportunity to reconcile our wishes, potentials, and fears. The dream is the mirror by which we see what confronts us, so we can initiate the first steps out of the original helpless dilemma of childhood.

In each dream described in this book you can see a bit of yourself—something of the universal desire to reach out, and then to protect yourself from the many fears, real and imagined, which confront everyone. In understanding the interpretation of each of these dreams you can know something more of your own dreams; then you will no longer fear and avoid them or regard them as alien or repugnant.

From these dreams you can gain understanding of your own inner nature. To know yourself better is to confront, understand, and gradually accept your innermost feelings. You thereby can begin to liberate yourself from the tyranny of unconscious "shoulds" and "don'ts," with their endless and unnecessary torment of punishments and worries.

In reading these dreams you can know better the deepest needs and fears of women, men, children, and adolescents. You will feel and understand the depths of what they experience. Regard each dream as though it were your own—an important inner message—and you will see things in yourself that are surprising and enlightening.

I

Women Face Their Wishes
and Fears in Dreams

Love and Death in Dreams

Love can be the ultimate success or pleasure. Unfortunately, too many people pay a heavy price for such pleasures. Millions of adults shun sex completely—almost like the plague. Most people have in some manner been brainwashed against indulgences in the bodily pleasures; if the pleasures are permitted, then the price of purgatory resulting from sin has to be paid accordingly. But this is only the beginning; wrongdoing in the eyes of the guilty is not just for the deed, but even for the wish, the fantasy, or the dream.

The child's fears are real and relentless—fears of being eaten, brutalized, humiliated, abandoned, ostracized. The child unfortunately sees all these castigations as deserved and carries his fears into adulthood. The list of "sins and crimes" committed in dream and deed is endless.

Both women and men are plagued in their dreams by the theme of both love and death converging. The dream appears to be an effort to face these fears fully—to overcome them, or at least to take the chance of being closer to a loved one.

Dream of Isadora Duncan

Isadora Duncan was a world-famous dancer of the 1920s who liberated dancing into free modern expressive movement. After her first intense love relationship, she had a dream while in a sleeping car on the way to Russia:

I dreamt that I jumped out of the window, naked, into the snow, and was embraced and rolled and frozen in its icy arms.

We can see this is the dream of a woman in panic who could be free only in the innocent fantasy delight of performing on stage. In actual life her emotions would literally freeze when confronted with the mounting anxieties of love, motherhood, and marriage.

While still unmarried, Miss Duncan bore two children who were accidentally drowned. Her later marriage to a Russian poet ended in separation. She died in France, accidentally strangled by her "trademark," a long scarf, which became caught in a rear wheel of the open automobile in which she was riding.

The original fears of Miss Duncan stemmed from a mother who in some mysterious way was cold, withholding, and threatening. Unfortunately, in her waking life, this dreamer could not overcome the grim forebodings of a cold, mechanical death which the dream somehow foretold.

It is odd that both Michelangelo and Sartre characterized love as "the fire and the ice." Goethe broke his engagement because he began to have nightmares of suffocating in a sack. The literature of the world is replete with the repeated theme of love and death—a terrible, unnecessary price to pay for such unrequited pleasure.

The lesson for mothers to draw from Isadora Duncan's dream is that you have to permit your daughters to grow into womanhood without panic or feeling the need to suffer. Mothers should be warm and firm and proud of their daughters' growth, without feeling jealous or threatened. A father should be warm to a daughter, but never become too close or so possessive that he uses her for his own emotional needs. Daughters who are plagued with excessive fear should not be so harsh upon themselves as mother was, actually or in imagination, or feel so deserving of self-punishment.

A First Love and Death

Although highly intelligent, a professional woman in her late twenties is very frightened and unsure of herself as she ventures into life and love for the first time. She has recently moved out of her mother's house—a mother who could be very dominating and threatening. She dreams:

"It is snowing. I look out the window. There is a path in the snow blown by the wind."

"Two candles are burning in the dark, eerie room. One candle falls down."

In the first dream we see the fear of isolation and the mother's cold rejection if daughter dares to challenge and compete by growing up and becoming a sexual woman.

In the second dream something worse is threatened. Out of the passion of the flame can come actual calamity, extinction or death.

In the Swedish saga Hagbad and Signe the romantic prince insists upon risking death to see his love, the princess of the neighboring warring kingdom. Before he leaves, he tells his mother his dream of a candle that goes out. The mother interprets the dream: "You will have your love but not for long." The prince secretly spends a rapturous night with his love, but is caught and executed.

The worst of dream warnings need not come true! But such dreams should not be ignored; they are signals for us to be on guard, to know and to face our fears and not feel harshly compelled to pay terrible prices.

Showdown with Mother: Kim Novak Casts Her Spell

A young woman in her early twenties has been much too dominated and intimidated by the women in her life—her mother and two older sisters. She is now just coming into her own socially, and for the first time she dares to operate freely as a real woman. These two dreams follow:

"Mother threatens to take away my sexuality. I threaten to leave home, but mother opposes this. I scream at her and, to express my anger, grab a glass pitcher and bang it on the table; it smashes and I cut myself."

"Jimmy Stewart enters an old curio shop. The woman behind the counter goes upstairs; in her place comes Kim Novak (from the film *Bell, Book, and Candle*). He asks to see a certain pen. She gives him an old quill pen. He keeps looking at her as he writes. It is obvious that he is now in her power—under her spell."

The first dream represents the showdown with mother —an artificially contrived situation where the dreamer in asserting herself as an independent, successful woman anticipates the worst possible consequences with mother. The dream also involves separation from mother; in the process, no one need be hurt by the dreamer's fury. She does not have to punish herself needlessly, as in the dream, and mother need not be destroyed.

In the second dream she is for the first time enjoying the full power of a woman—a Kim Novak, no less. It is the woman's prerogative to have access to the original magiclike power of the mother—to give all or to deny all if the daughter dares to take over mother's highly coveted role. There is no doubt that there is much magic in a woman's look, touch, shape, and sway—if she is not afraid to use the magic, even sparingly, to get what she wants.

To fully become a woman one sometimes has to learn to fight fire with fire. To defeat the witch one must, if necessary, be able to assume certain witchy (or bitchy) qualities—hopefully, not for any extended period.

The Dangers of Luna Park

A woman in her middle thirties has just come through a very painful divorce. She has been badly burned and betrayed by the man in her life. In a way she has sought this role of being the victim, as in the past she has not felt deserving of much better. She now dares to move closer to men but with great trepidation. This dream is the result:

"I and a girl friend with the same name as mine are with two men. They want to give us a ride on a huge swing made out of four large wooden doors. It looks dangerous to me. The ropes are not strong. They are out to hurt us. I refuse to go on the swing. There are many other rides that they want us to go on. I tell my friend not to go, but she doesn't listen. She gets caught on top of a ferris wheel. I scream for help, but someone says it is too late. Her head hangs with her tongue protruding as though she is dead. In desperation I call my younger brother."

What stands out here is her enormous fear and distrust of men, especially seen in play—really sex. This becomes a very dangerous business that can even kill. This woman remembers the rage with which her mother beat her when as a young girl she was once caught indulging in sex play with other children.

In facing the old fears, she is gearing herself toward wanting more from a man, but without suffering the old unbearable hurts. In the dream she is also better able to take care of herself, as opposed to the girl friend, who really represents the old victim within herself whom she is trying hard to be rid of. She no longer has to treat herself as harshly as her mother once did or as she herself felt she deserved. Men will have to treat her better from now on.

The Power to Kill

A newly married woman has brought her many childhood fears into her marital bed. She dreams:

"I am with my husband in bed. There are vibrations; the building is alive; I have to kill it. Suddenly the building stops moving. The witch monster is dead."

The building represents the witch mother who interferes with deathly threats in all attempts of the daughter to have her own man and enjoy sex. Childish nightmares still interfere but are being overcome; the woman, no longer so helpless, is able to mount a vigorous attack. The same dreamer, after becoming more sexual, has another dream:

"There is a crowd in the street. There is a valise. Only I know that there is a woman in the valise, suffocating to death. Only I know that I can do something, but I am powerless to do so."

In this dream we still see conflict as to how much control she has over her mother's life and whether she really wants her mother dead or alive. The victim in the valise also stands for the dreamer as a child, abandoned or punitively locked up, a helpless victim of mother's cold wrath. There is a reluctance of the dreamer to let herself go in sex completely, as this might finish off mother for good.

From these dreams, you can learn that many people (in fantasy) take their parents to bed with them, where clearly they do not belong. Initially, it is an unavoidable clinging to the parents out of fear, guilt, and longing. You can learn to separate from parents sufficiently so that as an adult you no longer have the need to bring them artificially into an adult sexual situation where they simply have no place. This then enables you to become closer to your spouse, without the old distrusts and shames interfering.

A Trombone Killer: Bathtub Play

For this same woman there are many continuing difficulties in sexual closeness with her husband. A most unusual and frightening dream ensues:

"A cold-blooded killer stalks his victim—a man. At first it appears that there will be no violence, as the killer comes in playing a trombone. The victim now also plays a trombone and in the rapture of the music closes his eyes momentarily; at that moment the killer strikes and strangles him."

The dream reveals the old terrors of total sexual abandonment. Men are not to be trusted. Intimate sex is so dangerous and forbidden that it becomes synonymous with death. Music (or sex), which should be for pleasure, is a most perilous undertaking. The woman's guard must not be let down for even a second.

This woman is facing her old fears fully, and in doing so will be able eventually to live as a free, fearless woman instead of being the terrified child victim who must watch every step, every move. The dream is a vital move toward opening her eyes more fully to old exaggerated fears, now irrational and out of place.

This dreamer finally breaks through her wall of dream terror and has this gratifying dream:

"I am having sex with my man in a bathtub at home. Mother and father come home and see us. I expect the worst; instead, mother speaks matter-of-factly about ordinary things. I am so relieved and grateful."

The dreamer is now clearly overcoming her worst anticipated dreads and is finally letting up on herself. Her life and her mother's life are no longer in jeopardy if she dares let loose and enjoy a man fully. Sex is now separated from the original dangerous childhood desires of intimate fantasy in the old family bathtub where everyone bathed openly.

You need not fear the worst violence of dreams. They reflect the exaggerated terrors experienced in childhood if we dared make a wrong move in exceeding sexual and aggressive impulses, or even thought along those lines. As adults we no longer have to cling to ultrasafe and innocent paths in order to feel secure. We can now afford to take chances because we are not so helpless and need not feel isolated and alone.

A Python Swallows Mother

A young woman with phobias of sexual involvement with men has not menstruated in many years. There is no apparent physical abnormality. She has this dream:

"I am about to have my menstrual period. Mother is reading a newspaper. A huge python swallows Mother."

The dream clearly tells the story of why it is impossible for this woman to menstruate. To do so, to be a complete woman, is tantamount to killing mother; not to menstruate is to save mother's life. Behind this "noble sacrifice" is really the original terror of the child that the mother-witch could devour her if she stepped out of line and was not a good little girl.

This dreamer has to learn to give up the old extreme feelings of being either completely omnipotent or utterly helpless. She is not the would-be killer of her mother, nor is she the little girl at the complete mercy of her mother's wrath. Hopefully, she can now take chances and permit herself the beginnings of womanhood without assuming the characteristics of the mother she could not stand. Becoming a woman does not necessarily mean destroying mother or becoming just like her. If only her father could have protected her a bit more!

In the Tree with Father

A young woman with sexual difficulties, contemplating marriage, dreamed:

"I am with my father in a tree. A lion comes. Father foolheartedly faces and outstares the lion and he is killed."

The lion here represents the extremes of frightening animal bestiality and sexual passion within us. Uncontrolled, it is death-dealing. In the dream, the young woman has the power to kill the man she loves; subsequently, she has to "kill" a real passion or intimacy with any man, lest someone die. The lion could also symbolize the devouring wrath of a mother out of control as she catches the lovers, a husband and daughter, in the tree. Father is destroyed. Who will now protect this defenseless "innocent" little girl caught playing with "fire"?

Peaches and Flesh

A woman who felt close to a man for the first time in her life dreamed that her son was eating a peach; it was smeared all over his face. She looked in the mirror and saw the same smear on her own face. She was then aware that they both were eating or sucking on a human being. She experienced horror and fascination, as though she and her son were vampires, like Dracula, sucking human blood.

Closeness with a man arouses the original repulsion of incest, and this becomes synonymous with death—with boing both the helpless victim, devoured or sucked dry, and the sadistic beast enjoying it all.

A Bird in the House

This is a dream of a young woman in a crisis of sexual closeness to her husband.

"In my house there is a bird flying all around. It can't get out. It is trapped. I fear it will make on me [defecate]. I'm terrified."

We see that she is afraid of her newly found instincts, afraid of giving them full, wild rein, afraid that she will suffer shame and humiliation if she lets go and loses control of her body in sex.

Somebody Swallowed the Cat

A New York newspaper reported a human interest item from a local hospital of a woman who had a baby and never knew that she was pregnant. Such is the "innocence" of little girls, carried into adulthood. A young lady who had a very vivid imagination as a little girl of wild sexual escapades, and of making babies, read that newspaper story and had this dream:

"I swallowed a cat. I didn't believe it until I was cut open and lo and behold—there is the cat."

This dream is a bit of a switch from the usual dream of the cat swallowing the mouse or the canary. However, they both represent the wish for stealthfully conceived babies, and then the fear of what will happen when these innocent "immaculate conceptions" are detected.

Dreams in which women kill their babies represent a denial that one had babies or even wanted them. Killing babies also stands for the victimized Medea in the woman who hates the man for his power to enslave, to betray, and to abandon her for another woman. The ultimate revenge is taken out on the children, but really upon oneself for daring to want so much—for daring to fulfill childhood dreams.

Embraced by a River

A woman expresses longing and appreciation for her dead mother in a dream and thereby frees herself from the burden of aloneness and danger.

"There is at first a terrible terror in the dream, as though I am trapped in a train tunnel, nowhere to turn, nobody to turn to, nowhere to hide. Then I find a river and am embraced by it and saved by it. The dream then becomes more like being trapped in a deep embankment near a river. There is a horse and wagon. I am not being pursued. There is no danger, and I find a way out of the embankment."

From the original utter helplessness and danger of entrapment she finds the memory of a mother to embrace; this enables her to save herself, to be a mother to herself for the first time, not resenting so much having to mother everyone else. This woman is now better able to handle

men, better able to take care of herself, to know what she
wants. She no longer has to prove and proclaim to the
world that she is the most deprived and abused little girl
that ever lived.

A Bird Is Born

The trappings of success are the hardest to take; to be
catapulted from seeming nothingness to recognition and
power is the test of all time. Here in the same night are
two dreams of a performer long struggling with the chal-
lenges of success, following her first serious winning bid
for stardom:

"In the dream I was asleep. I chose to go back to sleep
rather than go to church. My mother and sister enter.
They had attended church without me. I scream at them
with great rage, 'Why did you go to church without me?
Why didn't you wake me?' "

"I return to the college campus for girls with my sister.
I was happier there than I had ever been in my life. Why
had I left? I get out of the auto with my sister to join the
girls eating. I see that I am wearing only the bottom part
of my bathing suit. My sister is holding an egg. I see that
it is hatching. A little bird emerges. It is a beautiful owl,
so magnificent, with gorgeous colored feathers, an aura of
beauty. It was endowed with special powers as though it
had come from heaven. I feed the bird some of its own
egg from which it had hatched. It jumped around. A girl
gives the bird a rose."

In the first dream she very much fears doing what she wants to do, on her own, away from her family. This means being left behind while the favored sister has mother all to herself. There is also a pervasive guilt about not going to church—not conforming. She would rather be independent, and yet cannot stand the isolation and rejection that independence creates. The dream is an overcoming of the past.

Now, in the second dream she is ready to face the challenge of the present and prepares for a very bright future. We see a far freer spirit dealing with her peers. The dreamer is not afraid to compete, to shine, to be exhibitionistic, shocking, and individualistic. Miraculously, there emerges a beautiful, magnificent bird—a gift from heaven, the confidence of newborn flight and creativity. She is able to feed herself. The rose may be the harbinger of good things to come, perhaps permitting real love to enter her life anew. A star is born!

A Toboggan Ride

A woman who had been too fearful of sex lets go for the first time with her man. She then dreamed:

"My little daughter and I are going down a very steep hill on a toboggan. It is a new road with new grass along the sides."

The experience is all new and very daring. She is willing to risk the perils and pleasures which were so disturbing for her as a young girl. The dreamer is able to experience the exhilaration of letting go, taking chances, and sees that nothing terrible happens. She herself can now protect the child within herself as no one originally did for her, and so can be free to enjoy the prerogatives of a woman without the terrors and guilts of childhood interfering. In the process she becomes a stronger mother and closer to her daughter.

It is too easy for anyone to hang on forever to old fears and distrusts—to replay old scenes of betrayal, disappointment, and isolation. But if you really feel strong enough to take new chances, then anything is possible. Sexual blocks can be removed if you are ready to give up old angers and fears and permit yourself the exhilaration and satisfaction of new daring feats.

The Four Horsemen

A woman who has always felt deprived and is too easily hurt is on vacation with her husband and another couple. She feels neglected and left out because the others are engaged in intellectual "shop talk." She dreams:

"My husband and our friends are riding ahead on three horses. I trail behind on my horse, seemingly not being able to catch up."

The dream shows her unnecessary isolation, as though the woman dare not join the others or does not feel deserving of belonging. After all, in a dream one could wish for anything and give oneself all. There must be a purpose to wanting to be shunned or to feel apart from others, as though to nurse old wounds and indignantly proclaim to the world, "Look how shabbily they treat me. Make them feel guilty and remorseful."

This dreamer must learn not to do to herself what she felt was done to her in days of old. She can now control whether she wants to be alone or together with others. She has a right to be more assertive and demand more from others, if she no longer wishes to treasure her solitude. Being on a horse gives one a lot of extra power; she is not the helpless little girl she once was or would want to appear at times.

You do not have to continue forever the intense loneliness that unfortunately is the lot of many children. We all in some perverse way derive some painful satisfaction from reliving old hurts, nursing old wounds, making others suffer as well, and seeking revenge for old injustices. As children, we do not have the maturity to see the way out; but as adults, we all have our own horse to mount for greater maneuverability and power.

A Tragedy Averted: Going Great Guns

A woman is for the first time permitting her wishes to come true. She now can enjoy a husband, children, sex, and even resume preparation for a career. She has this terrifying dream:

"My young daughter has accidentally fallen out of the window, or it may be my younger brother as a child. I am horrified. I scream, 'Hold on to the building, grab on to the wall.' It works! The child is able to save itself."

In the past, success for this woman has been equated automatically with death; getting what she wanted meant paying the ultimate penalty. She no longer has to be a willing victim to these old paralyzing terrors. She now has it in her power to save herself, protect herself, be a good mother to herself, without paying the terrible self-punitive price for her aggressive wishes, which in the past she felt to be actually death-dealing.

She subsequently has these dreams:

"I pass an examination easily."

"I have enjoyable sex."

"I am playing baseball quite well."

As a girl, she could never hit the ball; this caused her endless mortification. This woman is no longer the inept little girl, the fearful loser. She is now the more assertive, confident winner who can pass all tests of womanhood.

No woman need be the inadequate and unloved child victim forever; but to break out of this bind you have to want very much to be the woman and give up the dubious advantages of the hurt little girl.

My Own Child

A young woman is finally able to separate from a father who has used her in a very dependent and demanding relationship—as his mother. She dreams:

"I am holding a young infant in my arms. I caress it, hold it close, and talk to it. I answer all its questions and feel very close to the child."

Instead of treating her father as a baby, feeling ever guilty for his welfare and devoting her life to him, this dreamer is now able for the first time to care fully for herself. Father will not perish, and she need not feel guilty forever. She can stop feeling so resentful over her plight and her father's ingratitude for her life-long sacrifices.

The dreamer can now be her own good mother and regard herself as a lovable, precious girl, deserving of time, patience, and concern—all that she never received in full as an infant and child.

The Cult of the Eagle

This is the dream of a young woman about to tackle large problems dealing with her fear of involvement with any cult, religion, movement, and above all, the fear of that "cult" embracing men and marriage:

"In a green field is a huge eagle cast in bronze with outstretched wings; it has to do with a cult power. I am appalled to see a thirteen-year-old boy taken in by it and being indoctrinated. They try to indoctrinate me. I scream for help. Father hears and runs for help, but is of no help because they seize me, inject me, and put me under."

The eagle, as the mightiest and most majestic of all winged creatures, is an expression of ominous divine power. In many symbolic paintings and allegories the eagle is depicted carrying away the hapless victim. In the Greek myth of Ganymede, a mortal youth of extraordinary beauty is abducted and carried away by Zeus himself, in the guise of an eagle, for his own pleasures. Of course Hera, the wife of Zeus, could not look upon this bit of erotic play lightly and reacts with due wrath and jealousy.

Both the wish for and the terror of rape enter into the dreams of all young, fair, and seductive maidens. If the fear is excessive, then all men will be regarded as much too threatening to be permitted close; hence the need to control them, keep them at a distance, and, if necessary, put them down.

In subsequent years the following dreams by the same dreamer gradually evolve:

"Somebody is robbing mother; she screams. I rush in and save her. I shoot the crook but then feel guilty; I did worse than the crook. I let him go, but I fear he will come back and seek revenge."

"A group of people want to fly. I am the only one who can fly, and do so."

"I tell off a cab driver who gave poor service."

"Jack Lemmon makes a pass at me; I am able to handle him."

We see that this dreamer has learned how to handle men, to be free, less afraid, and less guilty. The power of the cult has been effectively neutralized without the necessity of "killing off" the men. She has even surpassed her mother's power and is now her protector.

There is a strong reluctance on the part of today's women to being tied down to cultlike institutions of the past. The dreams show that no woman has to feel enslaved to any man or institution if she can understand the age-old fears and insecurities of woman that make for submission, and even that degree of gratification in being the victim. You need not suffer endless sacrifice for old desires, shames, and "crimes" committed.

A Turning Point in a Woman's Life

A woman who had a bad marriage long fears remarrying, for many reasons. In a dream we see that a crucial breakthrough to the next step occurs:

"My former husband and I are walking to the top of a mountain. We stand at the top; it is so very pretty and colorful. In the distance we see another mountain from which smoke is rising. Then we see smoke all around and realize that the whole forest is on fire. We run and put the children into the car. Close by, there is a cabin with older friends of ours inside—a man and woman. We can only save one person. The man has had a stroke; he is paralyzed and will die. He nods his consent for us to leave him. I lead the woman to the car. She turns into an infant, and I place her in the back of the car between my two children."

Our dreamer has been petrified by fear and guilt in claiming her just due in life. In the dream she is finally able to shake herself clear of a blissful childhood fantasy of caring for her ailing father, but at the same time she feels responsible for her mother's life.

Mother need not be sacrificed after all, even if her daughter dares climb higher into womanhood; more importantly, the daughter need no longer sacrifice herself. This permits her to finally give first priority to herself instead of living her life around her parents, her childhood desires and terrors.

In the dream, the infant is also the dreamer reborn, able finally to be a good mother to herself. She need not be the deprived child who forever sacrifices all for her parents and gains nothing except to feel unappreciated, unloved, and undeserving.

She is now beginning to seriously think more and more of remarriage, and though she knows that she cannot have perfection or guarantees, she is willing to take another chance—to regain some of the original pleasures of childhood as at the beginning of the dream, without the dread of repeated hurts, disappointments, and dangers. She may yet make it to the mountaintop—to stay.

How Dreams Serve Women

Women's dreams are clearly changing, becoming less submissive, and there is less acting the role of the helpless, fearful victim destined to suffer endless humiliation with its inevitable build-up of anger. Women, subsequently, need not take out early ordeals of injustice upon their men or children.

The dream itself is an instrument of this change, for it shows clearly what the fears are, thereby opening doors as to what to do about them. Just the act of remembering a dream in itself shows that we are ready enough and strong enough to face something important and do something about it. The dream shows the way and helps make the full woman—unafraid, proud, and giving.

II

Men Face Their Wishes and Fears in Dreams

Freud himself one day came to the discovery that the view of dreams which came nearest to the truth was not the scientific or medical approach but the popular or "peasant" one, half-involved though it still was in superstition. Thus, the unsophisticated have an unsuspected advantage in interpreting dreams; their feelings can be shown in full, directly, and not clouded by smart intellectualizations. The dream, after all, is primarily an emotional message and is not, or should not be, a mere abstract exercise of words.

We will now be witness to the sharp interpretation by a Navajo Indian medicine man of the dream of a white stranger. It shows that astute feelings are indispensable in the fathoming of dreams. This has important implications for all dream interpretation, but especially in the handling of the nightmares of very young children, as will be illustrated in Chapter III.

A Navajo Medicine Man Interprets an Anthropologist's Dream

Anthropologist Jackson S. Lincoln tells in *The Dream in Primitive Cultures* (The Cresset Press, London) how he submitted his own dream to an old medicine man on the Navajo reservation in Arizona:

I dreamed of a very large egg made out of a hard, rocky substance. I cracked open the egg and out flew a young but full grown eagle. It was indoors and the eagle flew all around trying to fly out, but it could not get out because the window was shut.

The interpretation of the medicine man:

The eagle belongs to the bird group of higher spirits which is one of a group of three allied spirits, namely, the wind, the lightning and the birds, all of which live on the top of San Francisco mountain. These spirits can wreak great havoc and destruction if offended. They can also be friendly. The eagle cannot fly out because you must have offended the bird spirit, possibly by walking on its nest, or perhaps your father had committed the offence.

The medicine man then requested that a certain fleshy growth be secured from the groin of a beaver and dried in the sun. He mentioned that sometimes white doctors had cured Indians where medicine men had failed, and Indian medicine men had cured white men where the white doctors had failed. The medicine man suggested that the dreamer return on the following day and he would hold a medicine "sing" to appease the offended spirit and give the dreamer a medicine drink as a cure for bad dreams.

At the "sing" the medicine man made a screeching birdlike noise with a whistle to attract the attention of the bird spirit. He then sang a slow, repetitious, rhythmic song. The singing grew in emotional intensity until it seemed to bring the spirit into their presence. The medicine man then struck the dreamer all over his body with a bundle of eagle feathers. Some of the herb-sprinkled water from the concoction brewed in a gourd was offered to the dreamer to drink. The aromatic liquid from an abalone shell was poured on his hands and rubbed on his face and hair. The anthropologist was then instructed to "blow" away the wings of the eagle spirit on "the wind." Four times the ceremony was repeated. The nature and tone of the singing then changed and took on a lighter, more airy, more released quality; it seemed to have the joyous sound of a bird soaring, flying to freedom. The bird spirit was now fully appeased; everyone was happy.

Interpreting the Medicine Man's Dream Interpretation

The medicine man demonstrated an amazingly nimble perception in putting his finger on the key to the dream: that the higher spirits were offended, that it had something to do with father, and that an offense had been committed. The dream probably relates to the inner inhibitions and fears of the dreamer involved in pursuing daring, innovative early anthropological research which attempted for the first time to relate dreams of primitives with Freud's writings on dreams. In addition the interpretation shows an uncanny awareness that the father also had problems with authority and that these "sins" are visited upon the son.

Pioneering in new fields of study is like fashioning new life, delving where others have not dared to tread, incurring the criticism and wrath of both authorities and peers in the field. It is once again like touching the forbidden Tree of Knowledge in that deceptive Garden of Eden.

The medicine man not only zeroes in on a highly intuitive emotional level, but in addition he has the advantages of knowing how to use every sensory function, embodied in intense song and flagellation, in a highly symbolic setting of ceremony, the spirit world, and magic. The usual verbal-intellectual weapons of the psychoanalyst are no match for this; before such an emotional onslaught the couch is outclassed and outgunned.

Love in Dreams

Symbolically, the greatest power attainment of all is in having sublime sex in an intimate setting with someone who is really important to you. It is only then that one experiences the original bliss of close physical contact between child and mother or, for girls, between child and father. After childhood one can only dream of these delights, and even then usually with guilt. It is when these past associations and hang-ups interfere in adult sex that there is trouble.

The extramarital affair is a living-out of the old forbidden fantasy and a pushing away of the dangerous or forbidden spouse who has become too close to the original home and is now, literally, mother or father. The affair is a compromise—forbidden but not too close, and hence "safer." In the love dreams to follow, note the continued connections with earliest childhood bliss and present-day sex. All real pleasures involve a regression and a reliving of delight, surprise, awe, and gratitude.

To the Magic Mountain

A man of great potential, but blocked in all his efforts, portrays himself symbolically in his first dream:

"I am a dope addict. How can I be helped?"

The dream reflects his inability to act. He is alone, literally paralyzed, and desperately needs to be saved. In his next dream he makes the first positive step to save himself:

"I have a baby boy. It has difficulty breathing. It is suffocating. I save him."

Years later he enjoys his first professional success and has this exotic dream in color:

"I am going up to the magic mountain. There is a castle used as an Oriental monastery. It is guarded by fairy-tale beasts—large elephants and many other animals. I use a ruse to gain access to the castle. I move in among the monks and am not detected."

Though in forbidden territory, he dares to act, breaking through to the mountaintop where there are promises of great beauty and many wonders. True, the ambition is still stealthful, and though he remains cloistered among the chosen few, he apparently finds friendly men willing to help.

In a recent dream he breaks through emotionally to a woman:

"I have a beautiful Oriental love. I have a lot of feeling for her."

From these dreams can be seen the growth transition of the helpless child to the giving love that a man has for a woman. You give up a lot in leaving the sanctuary of the nursery, but you gain much, much more in being able to experience full adult love, without the hang-ups of dependency, guilt, and inevitable disappointment that being the adult-baby entails.

A Witch Is Bewitched

A man who has permitted women too much of a negative power over him is learning how to handle them even if the means are somewhat drastic. He has this dream:

"A witch is controlled by a devil. I am the devil. The witch dies. I bring her back to life."

What better manner to outfox the witch than to call on the devil himself, with all the powers of the underworld at his disposal. Not only is this dreamer no longer under the spell of the witch, but he now has actual power of life and death over her—a direct reversal of the mother's original role. This dreamer can now afford to be benevolent and bring the witch back to life. He now has a new vision of a woman who can be trusted and enjoyed now that his own life is no longer imperiled by a mother-witch.

Being Eaten Up

A man who had desires for an older woman dreamed that he was eating a suckling pig with all the trimmings; it turns out to be a young child that he is eating, not a pig. He feels revulsion, but at the same time he nonchalantly continues eating, deftly using a knife and fork, as though this were the normal course of things.

To enjoy sex with this older mother figure is like having the original incest wish fulfilled, but it also arouses the original fear of being devoured, either by a smothering, enveloping mother or by a dragonlike father—the raw material for the making of so many myths, fairy stories, and children's nightmares.

To Impregnate or to Die

A man able to enjoy sexual intercourse was nevertheless having difficulty impregnating his wife. He then had a dream in which he was sitting on a chair. He crossed one leg over the other, but as he was doing so a bird flew up his leg and was crushed. He felt very disturbed by the incident.

The dreamer was later diagnosed as having a very low sperm count, which proved to be, at least in part, psychologically determined. The bird represents the sperm, which must be stopped at all costs lest it get through, impregnate, and expose the dreamer to all sorts of terrible things.

There is for this dreamer the real fear of suffering the fate of the unfortunate bird, which is as helpless and innocent a victim of its natural inclination to go places as is the child trapped by his impulses to explore, touch, and conquer.

An Incest Dream

"I am making love to mother. Father and brother are watching. I am angry that they are not bothered.

"There is an epidemic. I run around to get serum to make inoculations to save our lives."

Although the dreamer has his mother, what he fears is the epidemic which follows that can kill. He gets no help from his father and brother. If only they would protect him, control him, and curb mother! He desperately seeks to counter an epidemic which (like sex) plagues all and which is deadly, but it may be too late. Inoculations are like fighting fire with fire; this may symbolize more of sex, but in a different direction—away from mother.

A Fourposter Bed

A man returned to his parents' house to visit an ailing father. That night he slept in his parents' large fourposter bed, which they no longer used. As a child he used to romp in that bed with his parents. He dreamed:

"I was lying on my parents' fourposter bed. There is music. Mother comes into the room and asks, 'What is the music?' It is the dance of death."

The dreamer fears he may be as responsible in causing father's death as he was originally instrumental (in his mind) in gaining mother's affections and replacing father in the fourposter bed.

Mother Is Not So Dead: Homosexual Fears

A young man, too attached to his mother, contemplated marriage for the first time. He dreamed:

"My mother is lying dead in a coffin."

Actually, the mother was very much alive, but the dream was seen as the loss of mother, or the "freezing" of his feelings toward her. He had to turn the original dangerous or death-dealing passion into something safe, dead, and passive.

The same man is very much bothered by a homosexual dream. It should be emphasized here that homosexual or lesbian dreams are very common and need not be feared by those who are heterosexually inclined. These dreams are usually a decoy or subterfuge designed to deny or camouflage intense feelings toward the opposite sex which may be too threatening. For many people there is a real danger in intimacy, especially in intense and sustained heterosexual closeness. A relationship between a parent and a child that is too close can be terrifying to a youngster and carries over into all relations in adult life.

Homosexual dreams are also a natural expression of the original intense love that children have for both parents. Full love for a child means close physical warmth, which may later in life be looked upon with critical alarm.

That Forbidden Apple: Skeletons Under the Cathedral

A man who had warily kept his distance from women permitted himself a close relationship with his girl friend; they had decided to live together. He dreamed:

"My mother gives me a nice big apple. I bite into it."

For the first time as an adult he is able to accept the love of his first love—mother. This now enables him to transfer the old past yearnings to love for another woman. The forbidden apple reappears in a newly established Garden of Eden: the bliss of the original home of old is reestablished, hopefully without the serpent or a thundering godfather.

The inevitable repercussions come in a later dream:

"I was with a young woman in Austria, showing her where I had been before. They were excavating under a cathedral—an enormously complicated dig. Austria was on the border of England [land of his ancestors]. It was easy to cross the border into the beautiful countryside and rolling mountains. The excavation revealed an extraordinary find of skulls and bones and a pile of corpses stacked up like in a German death camp."

Digging into the past reveals the many ghoulish mysteries and all childhood terrors—being the helpless victim, abused in terrible ways. But one also relives old tranquil scenes and experiences of pleasure, followed by the ominous reminder of the grossly exaggerated terrors of childhood and threats of extermination. The holy cathedral symbolizes grandeur, guilt, and certain damnation for the many unpardonable sins committed in childhood fantasy.

Shaking Off Mother

This dreamer is beginning to realize his fondest ambitions, but self-destructive elements in his life have to be continually countered. It will be seen that the image of mother and son together is somehow tied in with power and success. Success may therefore prove to be dangerous. Two climbing dreams are presented:

"I climbed a mountain almost to the top. A woman was standing on a rock. It was very difficult to get to where she was standing, because the rock stuck out. I tried to climb the last steps to the top, but I had a sense of falling—of what would happen if I kept going—so I woke up in order not to fall. The woman was my mother."

"It was a bombed out church. I climbed up the large standing wall to a stained glass window. Behind the window was a woman with a child. I smashed the window with my foot and they fell. I asked my friend, 'Why did I kick the child off too?' He says, 'Because it was you.' "

The dreamer takes good, cautious care of himself by not pursuing his passions too far; self preservation wins out. He knows exactly how far to go and when to stop. The prized possession of mother is tempting, close within reach, but he knows not to tempt fate too much and not to push his luck too far.

In the second dream, in a religious setting of wrath, destruction, and danger, he finally rids himself of the tormenting vision of Madonna and Child—the ungodly closeness between him and mother, which threatens to destroy him. The dramatic vehemence and anger of the violent act shows that mother, though by no means out of his system as yet, is definitely on the way.

These dreams show how difficult it is to throw off those comforting though enslaving bonds of the past. And yet, to be truly free, the difficult weaning has to be effected, so that you, the man, can give more fully to yourself, your wife, and your children, without being burdened by the millstone of forever having mother too close.

A Bird in the Eye

Another dream is recounted by a writer who is fearful of making contact with a woman. He knows a famous man, T, who is very close to his mother but who has nevertheless married at the age of forty-two and has subsequently become a father. The dream:

"I meet T and his mother. We dine together. She tells of an incident where a bird defecated in her eye from a tree. We all laugh."

The dream is a powerful symbolic portrayal of indirect intimacy between mother and son. The bird stands for the carefree son as a completely uninhibited young boy. He could do anything he liked with his mother's overly permissive and perhaps seductively tacit approval; he could even fancy himself actually penetrating the mother. This age of innocence did not last long. It was replaced by his own excessive guilt and fear and by mother's stern, aloof disapproval and cold rejection of her young son's audacious liberties. As an adult this man then made sure that he would not sexually touch another woman. In part this was to hold on to his first love—but also to deny that he ever did commit any sexual "offense" against mother or any other woman, or that he was even interested in doing so. In the dream, contact with mother is at a "safe" distance without direct touch.

The bird droppings in the eye are really "hitting the bull's eye," discharging into mother's delicate "organ," from whence he was formed, to make a baby—an indelicate, outlandish, and dangerous business, certainly not child's play. Who knows what strange things lurk behind childhood wishes and later adult behavior?

A Rooster in the Car: Reunion with Mother

A man having difficulty becoming fully involved with women and who held back emotionally in his relationships had this dream:

"I am riding with my girl friend in a car. There are two chickens screwing in the road. They are scattered by the car. The rooster ends up in the car with us."

The dreamer is no longer such a passive observer of his parents' or any other couples' intimacy. He now has the power to interfere or break up the old unsatisfactory triad, and instead he places himself in the driver's seat with his own woman; he is now the new cock of the roost.

In a later, more dramatic dream the same dreamer has this frightening nightmare:

"My young son and daughter fight in the bathtub. I see my son walking out with an evil satisfied look. My daughter is lying in the water appearing to be drowned. He has tried to do away with her. I am horrified and call desperately for help, but immediately begin artificial resuscitation to breathe life into her mouth."

First the dreamer is reliving an old dreadful deed and guilt as though he did do something terrible to mother—symbolically killing her off or even ravishing her in some diabolical fashion and then attempting to deny or undo it all by destroying his feelings for her. He thereby kills off some of his feelings for all women and is destined to be alone.

The dreamer is now permitting himself to revive or resurrect the original closeness and passion with mother, which hopefully will permit him a new appreciation and enjoyment of all women. He thereby gives himself the chance for a new and better life.

An Ocean of Breasts: A Hammock Moves

A man who frequently had dreams of intercourse with his mother had an old recurrent dream of walking on an ocean of breasts. He said, "It feels like winning a lottery and having $50,000 a year for life."

Now comes a present-day dream after having really great sex with his wife:

"My wife and I are riding in a car. Both her hand and mine are on the shift together."

The dream shows a switchover from the old fantasy of endless breasts, of mother endlessly supplying all, to a newer giving and sharing with his wife. He now appreciates her more and is able to give more to her and more to himself, instead of the angry, passive, disappointing, endless waiting for mother to provide all, which, of course, she never does.

But mother's offerings have a tenacious hold and are not easily relinquished. The same dreamer has a later dream:

"I am ripping a hammock off two old trees. One end comes off easily, but the other end of the hammock is tied to the tree by heavy chains and cables wrapped around many times and grown over by thick layers of bark. It is a

back-breaking job to free the hammock, but I finally do
it."

It is possible to break that very comfortable and sooth-
ing hold from the past and move into a freer future. The
fruit of the tree is dispersed to root elsewhere, without the
need to destroy the original roots.

Milk and Honey and a Tugboat

For many years a writer felt helpless and blocked. Fearing
sudden death, either through overwork or too much sex,
he developed many incapacitating psychosomatic symptoms in order to limit his output and substantiate his
alarm that death was imminent if he made a wrong move.
He now dares to brave new undertakings and dreams of
his wife and then of a tugboat:

"We are having great sex on the grass—sweet as milk
and honey. It is a Shangri-la of beauty, color, and huge
mountains surrounding us—nicer than nature itself."

The second dream:

"I am on a big ocean-going tugboat covered over with
glass. I am part of a group. We are heading into a storm,
mountainous waves fifty feet high. It looks dangerous, but
the captain knows exactly what he is doing—slices right
through the waves. The boat remains fully upright, never
slows down, takes the storm beautifully. I marvel at the

sturdiness of the craft and the skill and confidence of the captain."

The first dream indeed shows great sex and closeness with the wife in the "promised land." This apparently lends the writer strength and confidence in facing the wrath of the oceans—battling with the cosmos, taking on the forces of nature itself. The dreamer expects the worst but emerges unscathed and identifies with the competent captain. The old feelings of helplessness are overcome. He is then able to face the future with more courage and confidence and goes on to tackle successfully the proposed ambitious task. He thinks it miraculous that he could have both full sex and full productivity in his work and still remain very much alive.

Many people are amazed that full sex and hard work in combination do not kill—provided that there is joy and satisfaction instead of a feeling of resentment and pressure.

Swimming, Suckling

A man was on the verge of full success. All of his dreams were coming true. These dreams followed:

"We are swimming in a small indoor pool, gracefully, rapidly, under and over the water like porpoises and then floating leisurely."

"My wife has just given birth to a baby boy. She is very happy and proud. The infant is suckling at her breast very contentedly."

Great swimming represents great sex. Then comes the baby. One can be father and son at the same time, enjoying the best of both worlds and recapturing the full bliss and gratification as of old. To give fully is also to be able to take and enjoy fully.

How Dreams Serve Men

Men and their dreams, as well as women, are also changing; they no longer have to be the perpetual victims of childhood terrors and feel restrained by the excessive bonds which originally tied them to mother. As a result, men do not have to take out their angers on all other women or their children and subjugate them as they were once similarly treated.

Men can be free to follow their natural wishes and inclinations without the tormenting fears of suffering violence, humiliation, or being swallowed up. In their dreams they face the worst of their fears, suffer the agonies of the damned, and feel free to release all of their murderous and sexual urges. Once some of these impulses are worked out of their system and they can be understood and accepted as the natural wildness of the primitive within, men can then feel and act as more civilized humans.

Dreams are the best evidence that anything can change. They vividly portray in action the means of effecting these changes, the right timing, and serve as preparation or dry runs for the new ways to come. The dream, if understood, helps shape the full man—not threatened, assertive, and capable of giving.

III

Children's Dreams
Are Very Special

We learn a lot from children's dreams because they are usually either very simple and direct in telling us what they want or what they fear, or else they employ a symbolism that is primitive, unadorned, and not too complex to comprehend. Very young children have vivid dreams—especially once they can verbalize. After the delight of their simple initial wish-fulfillment dreams, usually of goodies to eat, their dreams become more daring, but also more frightening.

Children's dreams always remain part of us; under duress we always revert back to childhood devices to seek solace and solutions.

Handling Children's Dreams

A child who spontaneously recounts his or her dream is also imparting a certain important emotional message;

this clearly should not be ignored and ought to be responded to in kind. Children's dreams are best not interpreted in an intellectual manner. A child may tell a parent any of these typical dreams:

"I dreamt that I was lost."

"You left me behind all alone and never came back for me."

"I dreamt that the whole family died and I was all alone."

What the child usually needs is a hug and direct assurance that he or she will always be fully cared for and never abandoned. The dream may be a message that the child is not getting enough affection or that the parents may be too busy or preoccupied elsewhere and that the child needs more of them. This situation occurs especially after the birth of younger siblings or after illnesses or parental trips away from home. At the same time, such dreams to some degree are inevitable because they are the beginnings of the natural separation from parents, especially from mother. The child is learning to be more and more on its own—facing and overcoming the initial panics of separation. Such an anxiety dream therefore may also be a "dry run"—a trial for more of the real thing.

Young children cannot differentiate between dream and reality and so take their dreams very seriously. They need direct reassurance in handling their middle-of-the-night nightmares, which usually send them screaming in terror to the safety and comfort of their parents' bed. Children sometimes whimper quietly in their own beds—too scared either to go back to sleep and face those demons anew or to venture out of the limited haven which their own beds provide.

A child having an obviously disturbing nightmare, with screaming, moaning, and much thrashing about while asleep, should be gently awakened, pacified, and reassured. Children need and welcome help in driving off those menacing demons, monsters, ghosts, witches, devils, and sorcerers. How can we handle any one of these very scary furies of the night? We can resort to a bit of magic—similar to that invoked by the Navajo medicine man in driving off the evil spirits: "Let's chase that nasty witch away. We'll teach her a lesson not to scare you. She is only make-believe, but I'll stay here with you to make sure she doesn't come back."

Once the child is deeply asleep, one can safely tiptoe out, of course, but not before performing a "checking out" of all possible "hiding places." This method is particularly effective with young children up to the age of about five or six, after which they should be able upon awakening to begin to differentiate gradually between dream and reality.

Where do these demons and furies of the night come from? Perhaps to some extent from stories of violence and television, but mostly they come from the child's exaggerated perception of parental angers and other sources of danger, as seen from the helplessness of a tiny tot. Children imagine and expect the worst. Growing up is a difficult, perilous, and oftentimes terrifying venture, and children need the constant support of both parents, who too often are prone to forget their own original unpleasant terrors and vulnerabilities; sometimes they would rather ignore or deny their existence and not have to face them anew.

If in the morning a child appears unusually subdued or frightened, he can be encouraged, but never coerced, to tell his dreams. In some primitive cultures it is a daily custom to have a "dream sing," to tell all, share all, and to release pent-up emotions, so as not to harbor and unnecessarily prolong children's nocturnal fears.

Freud's Childhood Dream

Freud had a nightmare about his mother when he was seven or eight.

I saw my beloved mother, with a peculiarly peaceful sleeping expression on her features, being carried into the room by two people with birds' beaks and laid upon the bed.

Freud awoke screaming and in tears, interrupting his parents' sleep. He thought that his mother was dying. He connected the birds with pictures he had seen of gods with falcons' heads, from an ancient Egyptian funerary relief. Also, he had recently heard the German vulgar slang word for sexual intercourse (*vogeln*) taken from "bird" (*Vogel*). Young Freud, just learning about sex, was apparently repressing his first obscure sexual craving which had found appropriate expression in this visual content of the dream, with considerable ensuing anxiety.

All Children Fly

Bert at the age of six dreamed:

"I was flying real high, just the way I am—I wasn't a Martian. Below me these people were fixing their car. I was scaring them—flying real low. All of a sudden they screamed and ran into their house."

Two weeks later Bert reported a second dream on a similar theme:

"I am flying in outer space, but then I say, 'I better get back because my mother may be worried.'"

The first dream probably reflects the normal omnipotency strivings and inquisitiveness of an active, bright boy. His desires and impulses to partake in adult activities terrify him. He makes it appear that it is adults who are scared and not he.

Bert's second dream is even bolder and more daring in scope than the first. He is now in outer space, but without overt threat or panic. A recovery has been effected from the terror of the first dream, but tempered by a wise self-preservative restraint—back to the safe regressed haven of mother earth. There is none of the panic of the first dream. Apparently in the short course of two weeks we have some indication that, to some degree at least, very powerful impulses and fears have been inwardly faced and integrated. From the initial omnipotent and scary thrust, Bert emerges both more daring and more cautious.

That flying dreams are already manifested in the dreams of much younger children is seen from that of three-and-a-half-year-old Cliff:

"A rocket ship takes me home from the playground. It goes very fast, too fast to go on the ground. It flies to my window, opens the window, and takes me into my bed. It's very fast."

Cliff has been having flying dreams for about six months or so. The common theme in each is unbridled omnipotence.

In Cliff's dream we also note the fascination of flying, speed, and the need to regress to a safer maternal haven. There is not yet any of the real terror that is reflected in Bert's first dream.

Childhood Dream of an Astronaut

Neil Armstrong had this recurrent dream as a child:

I could, by holding my breath, hover over the ground. Nothing much happened; I neither flew nor fell in those dreams. I just hovered.

What stands out most in this dream is a sense of built-in omnipotence and an equally marvelous built-in control system—the perfect combination called for in commanding the first landing of men on the moon. Here already at a tender age is a cool flyer who knows what he is doing and doesn't take unnecessary chances.

Armstrong recalls no dreams while actually in space flight. "As a matter of fact, if I remember correctly, none of my colleagues on Apollo Eleven were able to recall any dreams after the flight that related to any part of the journey to the moon."

It may be that the flights themselves are actually a living-out of dreams, hence obviating the need to dream during sleep periods.

Childhood Dream of Leonardo da Vinci

The earliest recorded flying dream of all may very well be the first memory of Leonardo da Vinci.

It seems that it had been destined before that I should occupy myself so thoroughly with the vulture, for it comes to my mind at a very early memory, when I was still in the cradle, a vulture came down to me, opened my mouth with its tail and struck me many times with his tail against my lips.

This may be the earliest recorded oral fantasy of mother hovering over the crib as seen by a most gifted child. Who knows but that it may be connected with earliest primitive beliefs of bird-gods descending from the heavens with their stern and magical powers to feed or to destroy—the life-giving mother, or the mother that withholds.

These children's dreams may reflect the growing omnipotence of the child necessary to master the necessary goals of breast, communication, and independent body action. The anxieties in the dreams also reflect a strong separation anxiety, which if too intense may regress to the unconscious, too omnipotent fantasy of union with mother herself. Then there is the danger in later life of the avoidance of adult success at all costs, in order to avoid the terrors of both separation and success.

What all these childhood dreams demonstrate is the inevitability of danger and anxiety accompanying their wildest desires. The anxiety may serve the purpose of keeping things under control.

Full Flight, and Then to the Moon

The same Bert who "flew" at age six has a much freer dream of flight at the age of ten, when he seems to show considerable sexual curiosity in an exotic island setting, after which he is off to the moon.

"Me, sister, and a few other people were living on a tropical island in the Pacific. We all lived in a nice big house. We were all birds. One day sister got married in a nest in a tree. She was very happy. She married another bird. I was watching the ceremony and looked into the nest. After the ceremony we were walking on a path, then we were normal people again. I was swimming in mid-air—like a breast stroke, but flying."

A wonderful dream! Pure delight! In a later dream Bert really takes off and finds himself the embattled victim.

"I had a dream that my rocket landed on the moon and two monsters attacked me. One monster was hollow—jumps on you and you're trapped inside."

One never escapes the anxiety of full free flight. There is always a bit of a price to pay or at least fearsome obstacles and trappings to encounter.

The flying dreams of young boys show the necessity and pleasure of making full use of their masculine prerogatives. But even at their tender ages they make sure they get back safely to earth and are not afraid to hold on to their maternal roots, whence, like the winged horse Pegasus, they could take off at will for new horizons.

The growing child may not be able to cope with mounting inner ambitions or parental pressures, which over the years become increasingly excessive and unbearable. Later, in adulthood, the actual achievement of omnipotent goals may pose real threats for an ego too weak to cope with earliest guilts and exaggerated fears of punishment. Flying dreams in particular seem to reflect the nature and strengths of these divergent forces at all levels of development because they are so closely tied in with the most powerful of children's fantasies.

Witches and Lions

Vivian, a six-year-old, overcomes prior nightmares of witches chasing and eating her; she now has a dream with a happy ending:

"Indians are shooting at me with bows and arrows. Then I become an Indian. A lion is going to attack me and then he turns friendly. We escape by boat and airplane. The lion takes me home. We live in a teepee. The lion is my pet."

Vivian is able to identify with her attackers, finds an ally in the feared lion, and in the end gets what she wants. Her dream is more open, direct, and successful in achieving her objectives than is Bert's.

The Family Jewels

Here is a most audacious dream of Mildred, age six:

"I dreamed that my best friend's mother died. I led the funeral procession down a street which went downhill. I was dancing to the Minuet in G, looking incredibly beautiful and wearing all of my mother's jewelry. I felt great joy.

"I awakened and realized that if I was wearing all of my mother's jewelry, it must have been my mother's funeral and not my best friend's mother. From that day I did everything my mother asked me. I remember that before the dream, when I was in kindergarten, my mother would trust me to wear individual pieces of her jewelry, but in the dream I was all bedecked."

Such are the ways of little girls; they don't want much, really—just everything. When "innocent" little girls are extra good, there are big secrets to cover up; mothers are so easily fooled. Or are they?

A Zoo Burns Down: Growing Pains

Children also identify very completely with the freedom and uncontrolled instincts of animals. Nina, a ten-year-old, had a dream:

"Daddy is a zoo keeper. The zoo burns down and daddy has to keep all the animals at home. The elephant kept sneezing all over me. I must have been drooling. The ants were creeping all over me. Birds were pecking away at me."

Probably the bodily changes and sensations of pre-puberty are already affecting Nina's fantasies in a delightful way—a veritable menagerie milling about the kitchen.

The simplified transparent symbolism of childhood dreaming becomes the direct free expression of nature's animation.

Prior to the above dream, Nina had her share of childhood nightmares; the most prominent one shows the growing pains inherent in growing up, of literally getting too big:

"The Nazis are searching for me and I know it's impossible to hide, but I try to anyway. I crawl into a cupboard that's too small. My legs are sticking out and I try desperately to get them in but can't. I listen in terror as they come closer and closer and then I wake up."

A Boy's Nightmare

A man came to dread touching anyone. His father had left home when he was very young, and the boy frequently slept with his mother for the comfort and warmth. He remembered a dream he had at age six. He is in bed with his mother when he hears the overpowering noise of a huge locomotive train rapidly approaching and bearing

down on them, as though the entire house and its occu-
pants would be destroyed. He awakens in terror, remembers the dream forever.

The train engine may be his own feared and magnified
power out of control, as though it would certainly destroy
him. The train may also be symbolic of the return of the
father, like an ominous dragon of old, vengeful and out to
destroy this young upstart of a son who has replaced him
in his wedding bed. The young boy was to live in terror
thereafter. The symptom of fearing to touch is the grim
reminder that forbidden sex can kill; the fear of touching
is a vociferous denial that he ever touched or tampered
with mother, a declaration that no real intimacy took
place between the two. It is the "success" of his symptom
that "protects" his life.

Of course, not all children verbalize their dreams so
readily, probably regarding them as too real, frightening,
and dangerous. They would rather not think or talk about
them, at least at certain ages. Children in their dreams are
already faced with the grim alternatives of kill or be
killed, so intense and exaggerated are their fears and
powerful fantasies.

Five-year-old Neal awakened fretful and not feeling
well; he probably had a nightmare. His mother asked if he
had had a bad dream.

Neal replied, "I don't dream."

Mother asked older sister Sandy, age six, to explain to
Neal what a dream was.

She said, "You know, when you're asleep and you
dream about killing people."

Neal retorted, "Oh, that. I always do that before I go to sleep."

The Implications of Children's Dreams

In dealing with children we have to cater to their sensitivities and frights; they are easily upset, but in their flexibility they can also be readily helped. They bounce back fast with but a bit of reassurance, support, and praise. Even a little affection goes a long way. The more you give to your child initially the stronger the child becomes emotionally and the less he or she demands. Woe unto the parents who do not give enough; the child seeks and finds retributions in thousands of endless ways over a lifetime, and the repercussions can reach down through the generations.

A parent is able to give a lot only if he or she has been given a lot. But one can always learn to give more, for in giving to our children we are really giving to ourselves and feel so deserving.

Learning to give more means giving up old angers toward our own parents for early felt deprivations. Giving more is moving beyond the need for the endless insatiable yearning to receive. Being able to give more also becomes an indirect expression of gratitude toward our own parents for what they were able to give us; giving then becomes a positive emulating of parents.

A wise teacher once said, "Wars will stop only when the battles in the nursery stop." In other words, excessive animosity between parents and children, at all ages, can build up and eventually make for pugnacious adults who are unfeeling, hateful, and vengeful.

For example, long, stubborn tugs of war between infants and parents about how long an infant should be held or left to cry unattended may be one basic cause for unnecessary fears, angers, and nightmares.

Honoring your children must come first, before the children can honor themselves, father and mother, other people, or eventually, their own offspring.

Being a good parent is no doubt the most difficult job in the world, because you are the only one who can do what has to be done, and it is so easy to go wrong. Parents constantly relive their own childhood and adolescence through their growing children and thereby are confronted with their own original hurts and angers anew and let them out on the young innocents.

The mistakes are not only in not giving enough but, even more so, in giving too much because of our own needs and reluctance to separate and let the children grow on their own. The dream can be a guide as to where you may be going wrong; for example, too much clinging or too much anger in the dreams of either children or parents could be a signal that things are too close. Likewise, dreams of bleakness, devoid of people, reflect too much coldness and deprivation and may mean that there is just not enough closeness, warmth, and trust to go around.

IV

Adolescent Dreams
Shake the World

The problems of adolescents are clearly related to their dreams and hence remind us of the extreme difficulty that this period entails for the youth actually in its volcanic midst. Many adolescents are perplexed, overwhelmed, frightened, and angered by the outlandish expectations of those elders who try to sit on them, ignore them, let them run loose, or use them for their own needs and gratifications.

No wonder that the usual adolescent nightmares involve the fear of being pursued by outlaws, rapists, or police, as well as cataclysmic threats of war, atomic explosions, raging fires, storms, and engulfing floods—all utilized to portray the chaos of the paralyzed victim.

It is so easy for adolescents to feel themselves the misunderstood victims, so alone and different. At times they cannot stand being at home, enduring endless criticism and having much too much expected from them, and yet they still need the security of home badly and are not ready to separate. We must let up on our youth in order to minimize their fears, guilts, and aloneness.

At the Controls

This is the recurrent dream of a youth, an only child, whose mother depended upon him much too much emotionally to fulfill the role of the old and infirm father:

"I am riding in a large airliner. Suddenly I am put at the controls. I am told that I have to fly the airship, but I do not know the first thing about flying. I am in a real panic."

This, clearly, is far too great a task for any adolescent to handle. It is inevitable that there be panic and confusion as to what to do with this newly found grownup power, responsibility, and sexual urge that have suddenly been thrust upon him.

If only someone could intervene between mother and son to ease the crisis. He has no recourse but to be the "bad" son in order to stave off mother's pressures; for him to be the good boy out to please mother and accede to her demands could only make for greater entrapment and disturbance.

A Vengeful Martian Presses the Button

The turmoil of the powerful adolescent instincts and their wild accompanying fantasies are best seen in this dream of a very ambitious sixteen-year-old youth who is break-ing ties with home and is about to enter college:

"In South Vietnam, at an American military complex, a renegade soldier has illegally pressed the button and launched an intercontinental ballistic missile with a nuclear warhead. He is seized and turns out to be some-one from outer space. In a demagogic manner, he is rant-ing and raving against all humanoids for what they did to his planet. He is on a suicide mission, sent to earth to seek revenge; it seems that in a war with earth, his planet was destroyed or ravaged. I am watching all of the action while flying above the base. I see the huge orange and white missiles, supersonic jets, and huge superstructure girders used to set up the missiles. I hear a British voice over the radio repeating, 'Westminster, Westminster (code name), this is not a drill! I repeat, this is not a drill!' I see superimposed on the Martian who is on the ground a ghostlike bat figure flying through space, which is what he really looks like. The ICBM attack is against all humans, but the missile will fall in Communist territory; nobody knows that it was fired by one renegade soldier and it could therefore cause a world nuclear war."

In the dream we see just a bit of the turbulence of youth and the enormous temptations to let loose, fortu-nately within the safe confines of dream fantasy. It shows the great inner struggle to control powerful aggressive impulses, with perhaps undertones of overwhelming sexu-ality. There are feelings of being very different, alone, and in danger—like someone from outer space.

The fears of childhood explode into the inner chaos of adolescence, to give a feeling of sitting on a volcano which threatens to erupt at any time. This is made more real, confusing, and acute by the ever increasing real violence of society and the greater threats of international destruction from the world communities brandishing their multiple atomic warheads.

The impulse to destroy the world is ever present in ambitious people who feel threatened, in such omnipotent and potentially destructive terms do they view their power. This dreamer looks upon his powers and ambitions as ruthless, like a Hitler, and therefore fraught with endless danger to the world as well as to himself. The desire to be the sacrificing hero is omnipresent, to avenge the "ravaging" of his planet and to indignantly rebel against the immoral world forces of authority.

A Modern-Day Mythmaker

A self-styled seer in his early twenties who considers himself a mystic with powers of telepathy and clairvoyance remembers a dream or vision that he had at the age of thirteen.

The dream purports to refute evolution, how man evolved on earth, and how the moon was formed. In the dream, he himself was one of an expeditionary force of thirty-nine cosmonauts from outer space who landed on earth about 100,000 years ago. They were to explore the surface of the earth only, but overstepped their bounds and began to experiment around with early forms of earth humanoids. This produced a strain of monstrosities which now constitute the present-day human race. And in their excessive zeal in tampering with the planet itself the cosmonauts caused the earth to go off its axis a few degrees. To compensate for this, a piece of earth ripped out and was flung into outer space; thus the moon was created.

This story was told in all sincerity as gospel; the seer truly believed in the events and in the part he played in them. His original story provides a wonderful clue about how myths of creation may have originated. From an analytical point of view, however, it is more than a bit suspicious—not that the dream took place and was accurately reported, but that the seer still clings to the experience and his crucial part in it as an accurate explanation of the creation of present-day man and the moon 100,000 years ago.

In actuality it is a denial of the facts of life, like a child stubbornly holding on to old myths as to where babies come from. The confusion of adolescents concerning their bodily growth changes and the many attendant sexual dreams and fantasies are understandable. It is common for innocent children and adolescents to both crave and dread sexual explorations, to take risks, to at least savor the fantasies of tampering with loved ones, to raise the possibility of impregnation.

What they fear in their minds is that terrible things could subsequently happen—like their being found out, producing monstrosities, causing deaths, and even toppling or destroying the world—so all-powerful do they feel in their thoughts and impulses. This fear of producing monstrosities subsequently plagues all adults as they suffer the uncertainties of daring to actually produce babies.

Note the similarities of this modern-day myth to the Greek myth of Phaëthon.

Phaëthon's Last Flight

Phaëthon, the son of Helios, boasts to his schoolmates of his mighty father's exploits as charioteer of the sun. They refuse to believe him and ask for proof. Phaëthon entreats his father to let him ride the sun chariot between the sun and the earth—a most dangerous undertaking, for any deviation or loss of control of the horses would pose a critical danger for the entire universe. The inevitable occurs; Phaëthon cannot control the horses with the necessary precision, and the world is in jeopardy. Jupiter, in order to save earth, hurls a lightning bolt at the chariot and destroys it. Phaëthon, with his hair on fire, falls like a shooting star and plunges into the waters of the river Eridanus. His sisters, who stand on the bank of the river, weep for him and are turned into poplar trees.

This represents the tragic fate of the youth who would seek too early to duplicate the powers of the father and ride the heavens. Here too is the overindulgent father who by exposing his son prematurely to the roles reserved to the elders resigns his own responsibilities, and in effect "does in," shows up, or eliminates the son as a serious competitor. The myth of Icarus has similar overtones; a son is sacrificed needlessly for daring to fly too close to the sun with wings fastened on with wax by his father, Daedalus.

Cutting Classes

An imaginative and sensitive adolescent girl has dreams of having sex with various of her men teachers in high school. She then is too afraid and embarrassed to go to classes for fear that these teachers will know; subsequently, she absents herself from school.

Obviously one can lose out on a lot of schooling with such sensitivities. This is a common fear of adolescents—that everyone knows what is on their minds just by looking at them—so self-conscious is youth, so overwhelmed are they by shame, guilt, and fear for their natural fantasies. The mortification of youth knows no end.

The Plagues

This adolescent girl has many phobias of heights and flying and has a pervasive fear that something terrible is going to happen. She has a series of dreams:

"Great fear of a poisonous snake and then rats running loose."

"Airplanes are bombing New York; most of the city is destroyed."

"My house is on fire. The fire is raging out of control. I run and escape."

For this girl the world is certainly a most dangerous place. There is the fear of her own impulses. She cannot accept the normal feelings of aggression and sexuality that abound in every person, in every home. She fears losing control; subsequently, there is the dread of inevitable punishment and catastrophe. She cannot accept her wild thoughts and impulses. It takes many years for adolescents to become reconciled to their own feelings of desire and anger, without the fear that anyone or everyone will be destroyed.

Understanding the Adolescent's Needs

Young people have to be handled with kid gloves at times and helped to control overwhelming impulses through a wisdom and patience that is never easy for parents or teachers to maintain—neither too harsh nor too permissive. Overpermissiveness equals indifference, abandonment, and despair. Youth has to be guided, not coerced, toward constructive endeavors. Above all, they cannot be pushed too far by expecting conformity according to grownup standards. Teenagers will goad and push any authority into punishing and disdaining them; this does not mean that adults should comply by falling into this trap.

What young people really want is some recognition that they are people with problems, going through some very rough times. Of course, adults may similarly be re-experiencing their old adolescent crises and angers, but in reverse roles; they take on the old harsh expectations of their parents, which they too could not stand originally. Domestic war then erupts, and the battle of the generations is on anew, full force. Of course, some battling is inevitable and perhaps necessary, in order for adolescents to learn assertiveness, set reciprocal limits, and rid themselves of angers.

V

Afraid to Live

In each of us is a bit of the Pharaoh, the astronaut, and the child. Each person has his own dream of what is wanted more than anything else; few can, or dare, achieve it.

At what point do our dreams impede us, stop being productive, and turn punitive? Probably when power, materialism, and narcissism become ends in themselves—dead ends—and full regression takes over.

It is then that cravings become unreal, excessive, desperate, and lead nowhere except to a meaningless void of boredom and passivity. That puts an end to the real dreaming of wanting more life, more action. Dreams that generate increasing isolation regress further into a longing for the return to infancy, to the womb, and finally to mother earth, as an easy way out.

Prolonged guilt and anxiety have a deteriorating effect on the body, leading to all sorts of incapacitating symptoms and illnesses, especially in cases where these innate predispositions or weaknesses already exist. The body's symptoms are the delicate indicators that something is wrong, that excessive psychic pressures are building up and getting out of hand and are simply becoming too much to handle. Since the dream mechanism is part of the body, ofttimes it will serve as the early warning signal that something is somehow wrong in the body, even before the clinical symptoms become manifest.

When one is too angry to give fully to others and to oneself, the anger can also build up into physical symptoms and incapacitations, as if one is saying, in effect, "I refuse to knock myself out any longer. Take care of me." Excessive reliance on drugs, alcohol, cigarettes, or overeating may also serve the same purpose.

The following dream is believed to reflect a psychically destructive process at work and shows the terrible toll it exacts on an adolescent girl.

Wild Horse Dream

Carl Jung was consultant in a case of a seventeen-year-old girl who was suffering from progressive muscular atrophy. Having to distinguish between hysteria and a fatal organic disease as the determining factor, Jung decided it was organic. The psychiatric examination revealed the girl's following dream:

A terrible noise breaks out in the house at night. I go see what has happened and find that a frightened horse is tearing through the rooms. At last it finds the door into the hall and jumps through the hall window, from the fourth floor down into the street. I was terrified to see it lying below all mangled.

This dream was preceded by another nightmare:

I was coming home at night. Everything is quiet as death. The door into the living room is half open and I see mother hanging from the chandelier and swinging to and fro in a cold wind that blows in through the open window.

Of course, a fatal organic disease does not automatically rule out hysteria as well. With her tragic affliction, the girl had good cause to be hysterical. However, such an unusual and dramatic dream suggests the possibility that, like Phaëthon, she could not handle her impulses, or perhaps the womanly roles which were thrust upon her, and was headed toward a tragic end as a way out. A horse trapped in a house where it doesn't belong. How did it get so high as the fourth floor? The fall seemed inevitable. The girl, like the horse with whom she identifies, may have felt that she was trapped, had no place in that house, and had to flee, no matter how. It is strange that a girl should identify with a horse, as a wild horse in a dream is so powerful, so masculine. Could the girl have been fleeing from a father whose own passions, she may have felt, were out of hand? Did she wish her mother dead so much that the excessive, highly punitive ensuing guilt forced her into becoming the victim instead? We will never know.

What we do know is that the emotional component in this fatal organic illness, considering the girl's very chaotic and violent dreams, cannot be discounted. The enormity of the anger and guilt in both dreams could very well have been too much for her to handle. Death could then be both a deserved punishment and an easy way out.

A Marriage That Could Not Be

A psychiatrist (H. Zulliger) reports the case of a young woman on the threshold of marriage who neglected her health. She had the following dream:

The woman is about to go for a country walk with her fiancé, when suddenly she sees a high wall, and a heavy black gate opens. She goes through in front of her future husband and hears the gate slam in his face with a violent draft. Thereupon, she falls into an abyss.

Four days later, on the date of the projected wedding, she died of pneumonia.

In another case a woman married late in life for the first time. All of her dreams had now come true. She had the man of her dreams, a new, beautiful home with all the extra trimmings, and wealth as well. Within six months she was dead of sudden malignant cancer.

Men who have climbed to sudden success, too fast or beyond their emotional or intellectual capabilities, may suddenly succumb to incapacitating or fatal deteriorating conditions or accidents.

One cannot help but be impressed by expert sportsmen, well known and successful, who for some unknown reason could not quit while they were ahead. There is the famous auto racer of many years who was killed in what he intended to be his last race before he retired; the same happened to more than one famous bullfighter. Skilled sky divers (parachutists) have plunged to earth without ever pulling the main or spare ripcords. Skilled skindivers have stayed under water too long and drowned. Are these all suicides? Possibly. But more likely these men were carried away by their own omnipotence and success to the regressive point where they lost their sense of judgment and precaution. Like a two-year-old toddler on the loose: "Nothing can stop me, nothing can happen to me."

Incurable cancer has for some people been called a "socially acceptable suicide." They just give up and look forward to dying. A significant number of these cases contracted fatal cancer just before they were due to retire, just before a future they had been postponing all their lives was about to become a present reality. They could not stand fulfilling their fondest dreams. The long-coveted Shangri-la was just too much for them to take—the old story of those "wrecked by success."

Emotions have long been linked with cancer, not necessarily in a directly causative manner but rather as an indirect influence over the ability of the body to fight any infection. Certainly, emotions have a direct influence on the will of a person to want to live or die. Any bodily illness strikes more readily when a person is under continued and unbearable emotional stress.

Why the Fear and Pain?

We may well ask why people who seemingly have everything are miserable, and why men make war and build atomic stockpiles when we could all be enjoying ourselves amid peace and plenty. Are we all like the proverbial Hungarian, happy only when sad? Do we all conform to Goethe's "Nothing is harder to bear than a succession of fair days?" A famous mountain climber wonders that such torment of the body should afford such satisfaction.

For those afflicted with both excessive desires and guilts, sufficient suffering and atonement may very well seem the hoped-for passport to forgiveness and eternal pleasures. But it rarely works out that way. Excessive guilt keeps the individual in his place and keeps him from interfering too much with those in power. "Thus conscience does make cowards of us all . . ."

The need to punish oneself is seen to operate most clearly in those overly ambitious leaders who actually acquire extraordinary power and live out long-cherished omnipotent ambitions. It is their abnormal craving for power that may very well account for the major wars of mankind, as compared to the benevolent leader who strives for peace without resorting to massive bloodshed.

The Price of Success

A man who has achieved some of his fondest and most unexpected ambitions dreams that he is trapped by two terrorists and cannot escape a terrible fate at their hands. In actuality, he has nothing to fear except his own inner torment of feeling the necessity to pay a price for all of life's pleasures and attainments, of having in the end to be the victim.

The fears of the past catch up with you precisely when

you are riding highest, higher than ever. Then you expect the worst to happen. If you are really tortured by too much guilt and fear, you make sure that the worst happens.

Steps Backwards: Making Things Harder for Ourselves

A man dreams that he is a little boy lost in the market-place, wandering aimlessly, looking for someone he knows. There is so much food and so many other goodies, but nothing for him.

In adulthood one need never be so helpless, alone, and fearful as in childhood. To be depressed is to be hurt, angry, to relive the victimization of childhood with all its many grievances and to enjoy feeling sorry for oneself too much.

For another man the prospect of success means that he will no longer be able to depend on mother, father, or wife for support. Moreover, giving up mother means moving closer to his wife—a painful loss indeed—to give him those old wonderful fantasies of mother. He has three dreams:

"Father will give me a lot of money."

"I am a little boy afraid to walk down the stairs by myself."

"Mother dies."

The first dream is the wish for reparations due; he then can forgive father and give up his angers. But what if father does not come through with the blackmail? Then the son is prepared to suffer, to feel deprived forever, never to be a good providing father himself, never to let father off the hook. "I am such a small helpless little boy; now even mother has abandoned me. Who will save me?"

The real loser makes sure he is forever deprived and alone—the ultimate revenge on parents who either give too much or too little and thereby create a demanding child that nobody could love, with the loser making sure it stays that way.

The Only Way to Live

One can always do more for oneself than one thinks is humanly possible. The resources within each individual are unlimited, provided we stop waiting for reparations for what was originally lacking, or waiting for saviors and benefactors to deliver what was once promised and is so long overdue.

The most satisfying surprise is to know that we ourselves can "deliver the goods" and that there are lots more where they came from.

There are many old superstitions to the effect: Don't have it too good! Certainly don't talk about it; don't even mention it lest your enemies hear of it and cast an evil eye on you, and that's the end of your run of good fortune.

To ride high, to enjoy, not to have to pay a price, and not to have to be a victim is the only way to live!

VI

Dreams That Save Lives

The ancient Hebrews knew full well the vital emotional and physical functions of the dream. The Hebrew word for dream (*chalom*) derives from the verb root "to make healthy" or "to strengthen." This life-preservative function of the dream is borne out by present-day physiological research, which clearly demonstrates that individuals deliberately deprived of the dream process become increasingly anxious and disturbed. When dream-deprivation experiments with animals are pushed too far, life itself is threatened. The body and the mind cannot do without dreaming; it is an essential part of sleep.

The dream is also a delicate barometer that shows the state of the mind and body. It is an early warning system to tell us that something is wrong somewhere and calls for action in order to prevent trouble, illness, or threat to life itself.

Fighting for Life

A shipwrecked sailor was afloat on the seas for three days. Exhausted, he managed to catch moments of sleep, during which he repeatedly dreamed that land was close by. This gave him the strength and inspiration to keep alive, to keep floating and swimming despite near exhaustion and growing despondency. On the fourth day he did indeed spot land and was saved.

Heart Transplant Dream

Dr. Philip Blaiberg, who underwent one of the first successful heart transplants performed by Dr. Christiaan Barnard, had these two dreams soon after the operation.

In the first, I was one of 18 men all on a train engine careening around a bend. There were greasers, stokers, the lot, along with yours truly aboard the locomotive.

In the second, I was at some secret drug-taking session. Here were these respectable men all lining up at a table buying drugs. Among them was a well-known Cape Town psychiatrist whose name I dare not mention. They spent every evening here, I gathered, secretly taking drugs without anyone knowing.

The first dream represents the power of life—going places but with an element of precariousness. The number 18 in Hebrew is represented alphabetically as *chai* (חי), which means life. The train crew is probably the surgical staff laboring over him. Dreams of walking or riding after heart surgery or heart attack are indications of the determined desire of the body and mind to keep that heart functioning—to live.

Dr. Blaiberg's second dream shows the apprehension that follows the creation of life using the heart of a person who is now dead, taking on the sacred powers of the gods. There is now guilt and fear. After all, another person dying so that one may live inevitably makes the survivor the recipient of guilt with the fear of punishment. Of course, following surgery, a multitude of drugs do have to be administered; but the secretiveness in the dream and the unlawful activities taking place leave little doubt that an operation of such magnitude carries with it psychological repercussions that go beyond the real dangers posed.

Those who survive coronary attacks and chest surgery have often been reported to dream incessantly of walking rapidly, as though the dream serves the vital function of a built-in pacemaker, to keep that heart and those lungs pumping. Behind this kind of dream is a strong-willed person who very much wants to survive, a person who appreciates life. When life is hanging in the balance, it could very well be that the right kind of dream definitely tips the balance in favor of life; it literally breathes life from the mind into the body.

The dream carries more weight than the conscious will because it reflects the deepest needs, wishes, and sense of worth of the person's unconscious; it is especially when the person is asleep that these emotions reign supreme and rally a failing body.

Vital Dreams in Concentration Camps

Here are two dreams reported by L. Wells in *The Janowska Road* (Macmillan) of an adolescent in a concentration camp who was assigned to the death brigade. These men were the hapless individuals, temporarily permitted to live in order to dispose of the gassed corpses of their brethren. It was only a matter of time before the same fate would befall them. There is something very real to fear—the grim inevitability of imminent death. The purpose of the dreams was to mobilize every bit of hope and strength so that the survivor would not meet the fate of the rest of his family, so that he would be one of the very few miraculous survivors of the death brigade.

I dream about my father and mother. They are crying because their last child is going to be killed by the same assassins that killed their other children. I awaken—I must try to escape.

At a later date he mobilized his spirits still further in another dream, before the successful escape:

I dream about the Seder night. The whole family is sitting at the table. My mother serves the food, looks into the face of every child with a smile. The candles are throwing a beautiful glow. Father is asking us children different questions. But I don't answer. I am only smiling happily.

There is little doubt that dreams such as these enable a young person to endure the worst physical and emotional suffering that could be inflicted upon any individual. It is as though the original full love of parents provides the potential victim with enough of a desperate wish to survive, enough of a basic confidence to overcome the worst of dangers and fears, and then to take big chances.

It would be difficult to conceive of a rejected or neglected child having the resources to care enough about surviving a death camp; such a child would be more likely to give in to death and to welcome it (not that many victims had the choice of opportunity or could be successful in their decision to resist, fight, or escape).

By those few who did survive the camps, there are reported repetitive dreams of home, loved ones, good food, warm baths, and warm beds. The dreams provided some degree of necessary sustenance or hope which reality denied.

Contrast all of the above dreams with the dream of a young girl who was awaiting shipment to a concentration camp and who did not survive. She told someone that she dreamed that her doll had to go on the next transit.

This pathetic dream foretells the preparation for the dreaded separation which she cannot prevent. The little girl identifies with the helplessness of the doll, and emotionally she is already detaching herself from other humans. She can do no more about her plight than a lifeless doll. There is no one to look after her.

A Dream Prevents Violence

A flier in a helicopter was having serious trouble with his superior officer and dreaded the inevitable showdown. He was strongly tempted to kill the captain and was even making preparations and plans to carry out the deed. Instead he had this dream:

"I am on an ancient huge sailing ship, a four-master. There is an ugly confrontation between two of the seamen which threatens the well-being of the entire ship. To settle the dispute once and for all there will be a battle to the death. Both sailors climb up the huge mast, position themselves at opposite ends of the main cross beam, and at a given signal both advance toward each other armed only with a knife."

The dreamer is a witness to all this from the deck below. He hears the savage clash of the two combatants, a scream as the wounded loser falls to the deck below, a sickening thud as the body hits the deck, and then all is silence. The dreamer awoke in a deep sweat, terribly anxious.

Could the dream of climbing to the heights and the inevitable defeat of one of the antagonists be a re-enactment of the old power struggle between son and hated father? The dream served a life-saving function by discharging the pent-up hatred and by reminding the dreamer of the terrible consequences of patricide. Needless to say, the dreamer did not carry out the proposed murder.

Dream Warnings to Preserve Life

We have to take our dreams seriously to receive both the very direct and the more subtle messages they impart. It is natural for many people to ignore or deny symptoms of physical ailments and thereby fool themselves that nothing is wrong. In the anxiety dream, the symptom may come through more insistently and alarmingly in the hope that the dreamer will perhaps now get the message.

For example, a dream of a heart attack, difficulty in breathing, or of utter exhaustion may simply be anxiety or punishment not connected with a real physical ailment; but it can also be a warning that something real is wrong or that you should slow down or ease up on pressures which may be excessive and too much for the body to bear.

Dreams do not fool around with unimportant matters; their warnings should not be ignored. The dream reacts like sensitive radar, imparting signals that danger lies ahead, and thereby automatically alerts you to take necessary care and precaution.

VII

Dreams of Scientists
and Explorers

Scientists and astronauts have a lot in common both in their dreams and in their actual lives. They are all curious and daring, and all marvel at nature's offerings. They seek to do what others have not done, to tread where others have not been, to discover the new and refashion the old. They are fearless in that they are willing to take chances, and while they all want recognition and acclaim, they do not shun aloneness or ostracism. The dream is a lonely undertaking, but the dreamer is exhilarated by his measure of loneliness and endures it gladly.

Kepler's Dream

This is a dream of the seventeenth-century scientist who was concerned with the early explorations of the heavens. One of Kepler's books was *Somnium* (Sleep), a fantasy.

Kepler dreams that he has bought a book and is now reading it. That book tells of a young Icelander who makes the long pilgrimage to an eminent astronomer of the day to learn what he knows about the moon. After several years he returns to his native island of glaciers and boiling springs. He finds his mother, who spends her time collecting strange herbs—a witch, as the son now realizes. He tells her about his pilgrimage and he learns to his utmost surprise that his mother knows much more about the moon than all the astronomers in the world taken together. She has had a better teacher than her son, because her teacher is a demon from Levania (the moon).

Levania is not inaccessible, but there are certain difficulties. Little demons are rampant both on Levania and on Volva (the earth). But they shun the light of the sun and they cannot cross space under ordinary circumstances because the rays of the sun would catch them there. But when the shadow of the earth touches the moon, they are able to race across this temporary bridge. And they return when the shadow of the moon touches the earth.

It is felt that Kepler's dream fits in with nocturnal childhood fantasies nursed by the light of the moon— impossible, out of reach, and dangerous. In the *Somnium* is seen his overriding desire to touch, to make contact with the moon. The mysteries of mother earth reach all the way from the nursery to that elusive moon.

Niels Bohr Dreams of the Sun

Niels Bohr, an early physicist exploring the makeup of the atom, had a strange dream as a student:

I sat on a sun of burning gas; hissing planets hung before my eyes connected with the sun by slender cords and slowly circling it. Suddenly the gas solidified. The sun and planets shrank simultaneously and hardened into a system of spheres held together by cords.

At this point Bohr awoke and suddenly realized that he had hit upon the model of an atom he had long been looking for. The sun represented the stable nucleus around which the electrons orbited, and this model thereupon took its place in atomic physics as a familiar demonstration piece. Of course, the dream did not come miraculously as out of a void but no doubt represented the distillate solution of years of pondering the almost insurmountable problems posed. But one can be fairly certain that along with the excitement of the "discovery" in the dream there was plenty of anxiety. To sit on a sun of burning gas is miraculous, omnipotent, but also quite dangerous; a dreamer takes the action in a dream quite literally.

Daring to face the sun is, symbolically and literally, the most audacious and dangerous of all acts. It is daring to challenge the awesome power of the gods, the father, the source of all energy, light, and life. No wonder that deranged men will deliberately gaze too long at the sun in mad defiance of authority and reason and thereby inflict upon themselves the tragedy of blindness, punishing themselves unmercifully for their challenge to the gods. Will scientists tampering with the powers of nature do likewise as they attempt to harness the energy of the sun?

Kekule's Dream

The chemist Friedrich Kekule, while investigating the molecular structure of benzene, dreamed of a snake with its tail in its mouth; this revealed the graphic ring structure of the compound he had been studying for so many years. Reporting his findings to a scientific convention in 1890 (before Freud's book on dreams), Kekule declared, "Let us learn to dream, gentlemen, and then we may perhaps find the truth."

First Dream from Outer Space

The first astronaut to report one of his dreams while in outer space was Gordon Cooper. While on an orbital mission he dreamed that he had failed to perform a necessary task in his spaceship. Cooper then awakened from his frightening nightmare, checked his instruments, and with relief observed that he had actually performed his assigned task before he fell asleep.

One can easily imagine a prehistoric caveman awakening terrified by a similar nightmare having to do with the vital task of tending his fires—the neglect of which could mean equally certain death, either by freezing if they had gone out or by attack by predatory animals. Hence, the possibility of the nightmare developing through evolution as a vital self-preservative function—a self-instilled watchman.

The nightmare of the type experienced by Gordon Cooper is seen as a way of cutting down on the dangers and unrealities of early and excessive omnipotence wishes, as a way of suffering or atoning in the process of victory so as to become more deserving of the final success.

Climbing to Peaks and Stars

In contrast to Gordon Cooper's dream, a total lack of control over impulses toward omnipotence is reflected in the dream of a mountain-climbing colleague reported by Jung:

> I am climbing a high mountain over steep, snow covered slopes. I mount higher and higher—it is marvelous weather. The higher I climb, the better I feel. I think: if only I could go on climbing like this for ever! When I reach the summit, my happiness and elation are so strong that I feel I could mount right up into space. And I discover that I actually can do this. I go on climbing on empty air. I awake in a real ecstasy.

Jung anxiously implored his colleague to give up mountain climbing, but to no avail: He fell to his death three months later in his last tangle with a destiny that he could not forsake.

The tragic portent of Jung's mountain climber's dream may be an uncontrolled take-off on Jacob's ladder dream, in which our Biblical hero dreams of an actual walkable bridge up to the inaccessible and desirable heavens themselves. God's omnipotent ways and feats are made known to a mortal. Each year large numbers of men die climbing mountains. What starts out as an exhilarating brush with nature's pleasures ends in stark tragedy. Even in the successful ascent designed ostensibly for pleasure, there is usually an inordinate degree of suffering and gruelling effort hardly compatible with leisurely pursuits. In reading accounts of mountain climbers and their ordeals, one is struck by the magnitude of the prolonged mental and physical anguish to which these men subject themselves in an unending series of bouts with blinding snowstorms and wet, freezing, sleepless nights, with agonizing pain and exhaustion, and then the torment of injuries, frozen limbs, amputations, and death. Why such pain?

The feelings of omnipotence in the young child are the makings of a little dictator or monster who wants and may even get all. Like all dictators, he must also suffer the consequences of his overextended lust, and he builds up within himself those very limitations and flaws that will guarantee his partial or complete downfall—either in the interests of self-preservation, or for a deserved self-inflicted annihilation. Dare we make the connection between omnipotent strivings on the one hand and, on the other hand, the risk of life and limb to fulfill childhood yearnings of conquering, possessing a long-cherished mother, or reliving the complete bliss of having all? Do warrior conquerors and conquerors of mountains have something in common? Here are some direct quotations of famous mountain climbers who succeeded—where many of their predecessors had failed and died—in the final conquering of the summits of Annapurna, the Matterhorn, Mont Blanc, and Mount McKinley.

It became for me a kind of illness. I could not even look upon the mountain, which is visible from so many points round about, without being seized with an aching of desire.

Only those who have for long years cherished a great and almost inordinate desire, and have had that desire gratified . . . can enter into the deep thankfulness and content that filled the heart . . .

I was weak under the weight of emotion. I had to sit down on a little rock to savor my happiness awhile. I realized I had come home. My lost horizon, the life which I thought had been destroyed, were returned to me in full. Once more my friends— the glaciers, even the rocks—spoke to me in their affectionate tongue. At that moment I felt that the long ordeal was over. I felt like a man.

Dreams Make for Daring Feats

People need not fear their ambitions or pay terrible prices for the realization of their fondest dreams. The dream tells us how far or high to go in safety. The message of the dream must be heeded, lest there be actual peril to life itself.

The dream is our best gauge as to when to let up and when to proceed, bearing in mind that there are always inevitable exaggerated anxieties connected with ambition and new undertakings. Some false alarms are to be anticipated, making for needless, blocked efforts, but the more one knows oneself the more one is able to distinguish the real warning from the unfounded anxiety, and so act accordingly.

VIII

Dreams of Writers and Painters

Fortunately, war and violence are not the sole recourse for those zealots who are hell-bent on conquering mother earth. There are more peaceful, though not necessarily safer, means of attaining one's objective.

Writers and painters also attempt to encompass, dominate, or refashion the world in some manner or other. However, even their peaceful pursuits, if excessive, can prove calamitous.

In highly prolific writers such as Balzac and Thomas Wolfe, we see in operation an obsession for fame and power which hints at a self-destructive overproductivity. Virtually all of Balzac's favorite heroes in his novels were destined to be destroyed by their own corrupt passions: Balzac and Wolfe in their own times suffered similar fates because through neglect they impaired their health. Both authors had created Frankenstein monsters in their many works; the monsters ultimately got out of hand and destroyed their creators.

In *Of Time and the River* Wolfe describes Eugene Gant, the student:

He simply wanted to know everything on earth; he wanted to devour the earth, and it drove him mad when he saw he could not do this.

Balzac and Wolfe were to achieve their long-awaited fame, but this did little to assuage their dissatisfaction or diminish their relentless drive. Wolfe expressed these feelings in *You Can't Go Home Again:*

And all the while, of course, I was still enamored of that fair Medusa, Fame. My desire for her was a relic of the past. All the guises of Fame's loveliness—phantasmal, ghostwise, like something flitting in a wood—I had dreamed of since my early youth until her image and the image of the loved one had a thousand times been merged together. I had always wanted to be loved and to be famous. Now I had known Love, but Fame was still elusive. So in the writing of the second book, I courted her.

So with Fame. In the end, I had to have her. She was another woman—of all Love's rivals, as I was to find by a strange paradox, the only one by women and by Love beloved. And I had her, as she may be had—only to discover that Fame, like Love, was not enough.

Fame apparently represents man's long-sought cherished dream of being continually in the limelight, being fully recognized and loved, and recapturing the blissful, omnipotent position of his early life with mother. But as with any unfulfilled childhood need, it defies long-lasting gratification in adulthood. Success and fame do not suffice.

A *Flying Dream of Dylan Thomas*

Here is a repetitive flying dream of Dylan Thomas:

I am back at my Welsh dame's school, and reveal to my friends that at last I have a real secret. I can fly. And when they do not believe me, I flap my arms and slowly leave the ground only a few inches at first, then gaining air until I fly waving my cap level with the upper windows of the school, peering in until the mistress at the piano screams and the metronome falls to the ground and stops, and there is no more time.

And I fly over the trees and chimneys of my town, over the dockyards skimming the masts and funnels, over Inkerman Street and Sebastopol Street, and the street where all the women wear men's caps, over the trees of the everlasting park, where a brass band shakes the leaves and sends them showering down onto the nurses and the children, the cripples and the idlers, and the gardeners, and the shouting boys: over the yellow seashore, and the stone-chasing dogs, and the old men, and the singing sea. The memories of childhood have no order, and no end.*

Dylan Thomas's wonderfully creative poems were unfortunately cut short when he reached the age of thirty-nine by the excesses of his omnipotent indulgences.

There is a striking similarity between children's flying

* *The Griffin*, Volume 9, Number 8, Readers Subscription, Inc.

dreams and the above dream of Dylan Thomas. They all express amazement and fascination with their own bodies in their newly found magical ability to fly. The daring dreams of children invariably involve an element of terror which stops the dream cold—it ends on that note of acute anxiety. This is not the case with Dylan Thomas; from the terror of the frightened school mistress, he blithely continues his leisurely flight over the rest of the town, admiring its many colorful and delightful scenes and people. Nothing seems to bother or stop Dylan Thomas in the dream or in life.

Contrasting the Jacob's ladder dream to both Dylan Thomas's dream and Jung's account of the mountain-climbing dreamer who fell to his death, we see that the ladder serves as a very clever built-in device of safety and control; one foot is literally kept on the ground, while the other foot dares to soar.

Maxim Gorky: Two Dreams

I saw the sky, scrofulous, putrescent, greenish-yellow, and the stars in it were round, flat, without rays, without luster, like scabs on the skin of a diseased person. And there glided across this putrescent sky, slowly, reddish forked lightning, rather like a snake, and when it touched a star, the star swelled up into a ball and burst noiselessly, leaving behind it a darkish spot, like a little smoke; and then the spot vanished quickly in the bleared and liquid sky. Thus all the stars one after another burst and perished, and the sky, growing darker and more horrible, at last whirled upwards, bubbled, and bursting into fragments began to fall on my head in a kind of cold jelly, and in the spaces between the fragments there appeared a shiny blackness as though of iron.

A snowy plain, smooth like a sheet of paper; no hillock, no tree, no bush anywhere, only—barely visible—a few rods poked out from under the snow. And across the snow of this dead desert, from horizon to horizon, there stretched a yellow strip of hardly distinguishable road, and over the road there marched slowly a pair of gray felt-top boots—empty.

Gorky, a pen name, means "the bitter one." His life was indeed bitter, for when he was five years old his father died. His mother remarried, and young Gorky was brought up in poverty by his grandparents. He went to work at the age of eight. Such were the terrible prices he may have felt he had to pay for his earliest dreams of who knows what. From these bitter experiences were to spring great works like *The Lower Depths, Mother,* and *Enemies.*

In Gorky's dreams, mingled with the magnificence and grandeur of the heavens, disease and a nightmarish cataclysm of all the destructive forces of nature are let loose. It is indeed perilous to tread and touch in such exalted realms of nature.

The second dream may represent the consequences of the world-shattering ambitious thirst of the first dream. Here we see coldness and desolateness, and the pair of empty marching boots may very well symbolize the death of his father, perhaps even fearful anticipations of his own death.

Marc Chagall Dreams

Marc Chagall recounts a dream in his autobiography, *My Life* (Orion Press). During the preceding day, the artist couldn't stand his child's cries. "People will say I'm a monster!" he exclaimed. He then dreams:

A little bitch bit out Idotchka. It was night. Through my bedroom window I saw the vault of the sky crossed by gigantic, multicolored squares, by rounds, meridians, streaked with written signs. Moscow, stop—Berlin, stop—New York, stop— Rembrandt, Vitebsk. Millions of agonies. All the colors except ultramarine, smoulder and burn. I turn around and I see my picture in which men are beside themselves, frantic. It was hot. Everything looked green. I lie between those two worlds, looking out of the window. The sky is not blue now and at night it sings like a seashell and shines more brilliantly than the sun.

Could that dream have been a portent of my dash across the field the next day when my little girl fell and was hurt.

In the dream we see an enormous creative thrust toward the heavens creating something even more brilliant than the sun. It all springs from the dog biting his daughter. Could this be the wildness of the young boy possessively sinking his teeth into mother? But there are millions of agonies to pay—which perhaps all artists have to pay for such daring exploits and creations—to outdo nature itself, to show up the gods, to possess the earth.

Thereafter, Chagall's paintings were to become silent, visually fixed dreams of his earliest loves and memories for everyone to view forever. He could, in accepting and enjoying this pastoral repose, go on to enjoy a long, ever more productive life, in contrast to the short-lived creativity of Dylan Thomas. Thomas's life, despite his creative exuberance, lacked real control and direction; seemingly nothing bothered him and nothing stopped him, and yet he made himself pay too high a price for his excesses.

J. B. Priestley Dreams

J. B. Priestley's plays are concerned with social criticism and the meaning of time. He dreamed:

I was standing at the top of a very high tower, alone, looking down upon myriads of birds all flying in one direction; every kind of bird was there, all the birds in the world. It was a noble sight, this vast aerial river of birds. But now in some mysterious fashion the gear was changed, and time speeded up, so that I saw generations of birds, watched them break their shells, flutter into life, weaken, falter, and die. Wings grew only to crumble; bodies were sleek and then, in a flash, bled and shrivelled; and death struck everywhere at every second. . . . As I stared down, seeming to see every creature's ignoble little history almost at a glance, I felt sick at heart. . . . I stood on my tower, still alone, desperately unhappy. But now the gear was changed again and time went faster still, and it was rushing by at such a rate that the birds could not show any movement but were like an enormous plain sown with feathers. But along this plain, flickering through the bodies themselves, there now passed a sort of white flame, trembling, dancing, then hurrying on; and as soon as I saw it I knew that this flame was life itself, and then it came to me, in a rocket-burst of ecstasy, that nothing mattered, because nothing else was real, but this quivering and hurrying lambency of being. Birds, men, or creatures . . . all were of no account except so far as this flame of life travelled through them. It left nothing to mourn over behind it; what I had thought was tragedy was mere emptiness or a shadow show; for now all real feeling was caught and purified and danced on ecstatically with the white flame of life. I had never felt before such deep happiness as I knew at the end of my dream of the tower and the birds.*

This very powerful dream deals with the generations of life, power, procreation, and death. From his lonely perch, Priestley seeks meaning and direction in life, finding it in the white flame—the eternal flame, which is life itself, being immortal, never-ending, and therefore purposeful. It is then that he is not alone and can feel deep happiness. The dream is also an overcoming of the fear to create— facing the deepest threats involved in cutting loose and daring to soar, to take chances, and thereby to symbolically risk death.

The dream seems like the nearly immortal phoenix rising from the ashes to be reborn, symbolic of death and resurrection. The white flame of the dream, "trembling, dancing, then hurrying on," has the ring of passion and therefore may be symbolic of procreation—the magic of birth or new writings. With this, the threat of death or being burned up turns instead into new life, death, and rebirth. This is what the dream is all about. What a wonderful way to counter death!

* J. B. Priestley, *Man and Time*, Doubleday.

A Painter's Dilemma

A successful contemporary painter has just made some important sales, and a new exhibit is about to open. He has this dream:

"I am talking to a brash, argumentative student at a party. He takes a pamphlet out of my bookcase, examines it, and says, 'You should take this and sell it, it's very valuable.' I say, 'Why don't you stop telling me what I should do?' There is a fracas. I tell him to leave the party. He goes—seems downcast. I catch him in the hall and tell him to return if he wishes; I've overreacted.

"I am back in the room with my girl. There is a robin's egg on the table (as though for display or for someone's collection—not to be mishandled). I pick up the egg without wishing to and bite into it by mistake. I gag; the texture or something is very unpleasurable. I throw it into a cradle-shaped garbage container and try to hide the deed from my girl by covering the egg with a used paper towel. I see a fetus develop from the egg into a chick. Without wanting to, but in desperation, I try to step on it with my foot; it gives an alarming screeching noise. I now realize that there is another chicken in the container. It is fully developed like a mother hen, but the size of a chick. I try to step on it too; although I smash it and draw blood, I can't seem to kill either bird or stop their clamoring."

It is very difficult for the dreamer to accept his success or creativity. It springs up all around him, but he cannot let go of it; he tries to squelch it, but to no avail. It is like trying to stamp out sex; it will not go away.

He has to accept his impulses, his earliest desires, and not let them interfere with his work. He cannot and need not kill off the mother within; she remains an intrinsic force of instinct and creativity from which to draw fully and gladly. The natural maternal component of aesthetics and productivity never killed anyone and need not pose any great threat.

To create paintings is, for him, like making babies (symbolized by biting into the egg on display and its subsequent hatching). Everyone will now see and know; the child in him dreads the worst consequences of the deed. He tries to erase all evidences of procreation, but it doesn't work.

He identifies with the young birds—their puniness and helplessness, as victims under the feet of their tormentor —at the same time that he is the harsh, ruthless punisher of himself. No one can stand the free, delightful bird within, least of all himself.

He dare not be great or impregnate, but he is finally coming to accept the fact that there need be nothing dangerous or forbidden about creation and success and that it need not destroy him.

The Flying Painter

A young painter is struggling to develop his own style but is far from satisfied; self-doubt has always plagued him. This is his dream:

"I am painting the walls of my room. The shades of paint are off and the height of the walls is not right. It seems that the work can never turn out right. I have the ability to fly as I paint, being able to hover over the walls; I can also walk up and down the walls with my suction-like feet. My girl friend standing below tries to help but is of no help. I notice grease smudges on the wall which I missed previously."

This painter wavers between the unsatisfactory extremes of being either the omnipotent, talented genius with super powers, or else he seeks a guru, a patron, or a mother protector to take him under their wings, show him everything, and guide him through to success. For the first time he now finds these extremes unfeasible and impossible of attainment. He is giving up perfectionistic and impossible goals; more and more he is relying upon his own hard efforts and is becoming more critical and objective toward his work.

The Dreamer Grounded

We have seen the joys and perils of flying dreams and how even children's dreams already institute safety devices for "grounding" their unbridled power. This would presuppose an internalization of proper controls initiated from without from parents. It may therefore follow that the greater the unchecked omnipotence in adult flying dreams, the greater the weakness of an underdeveloped ego to institute necessary controls, and the greater may be the seeking of self-destruction because one may feel deserving of it. It may be a desperate attempt to ground oneself.

The excessive anxiety generated can easily lead to compulsive acting out, be it in the area of dangerous mountain climbing or any excessive addiction. Where there is no impulse control, the need to topple or punish oneself becomes paramount (like "Stop me before I murder again").

Jacob's ladder dream shows how old is the protective device of keeping the dreamer "grounded." This may also be reflected in the general symbolic appearance of horses, automobiles, ships, etc., in dream actions, which would still encompass the spirit of disembodied power and speed but in a more controlled and less omnipotent fashion. Thus Freud's personal reported dreaming reached its zenith of omnipotence in a dream in which he was riding on a gray horse; this dream was soon followed by the non-visual dream in which the Pope was dead. At the time of the first dream, Freud had been suffering from boils which made every moment torture, and finally a boil the size of an apple had risen at the base of his scrotum, which caused almost unbearable pain with every step he took. This occurred shortly before his father's death; for his desired omnipotent and imminent ascension to his father's role, Freud really "grounded" himself with a punitive, incapacitating, but still "safe" symptom.

The problem of handling omnipotent fantasies has become more crucial than ever, not only for the individual but for the very survival of mankind. The scientists and the politicians now possess much greater omnipotent power than the ability to fly. To orbit the earth, to land on the moon, or to be able to atomize all life on earth outdoes the awesome power of Zeus himself. This may very well generate far more guilt-punishment panic than pure fantasy or dream. What the conscious achieves and produces in reality, the unconscious may ruthlessly undo and destroy unless man can accept his wildest dreams—and then enjoy and control his most omnipotent deeds. The flying dream may show the way.

IX

Dreams of Warriors and Heroes

The *Epic of Gilgamesh* is an early Babylonian equivalent of the *Odyssey*. This epic of our earliest hero goes back perhaps four thousand years; the remains of its twelve tablets were unearthed in this century and the last, chiefly in the temple library of an Assyrian king. Gilgamesh is the true folk hero. He rises to power with the aid of his trusted companion Enkidu to serve his people; he slays the monsters representing tyranny and evil, unsuccessfully seeks immortality, and in the end—like all mortals—dies. In this epic are the oldest recorded dreams in history.

The first dream of Gilgamesh in the old Babylonian version is reported to his mother:

Gilgamesh arose to reveal the dream,
Saying to his mother:
"My mother, last night
I felt happy and walked about

Among the heroes
There appeared stars in the heavens
[The h]ost of heaven fell down toward me
I tried to lift it, but it was too heavy for me;
I tried to move it, but I could not move it.
The Land of Uruk was gathered around it,
While the heroes kissed its feet
I put my forehead (firmly) against (it),
And they assisted me.
I lifted it up and carried it to thee."
The mother of Gilgamesh, who is versed in everything,
Says to Gilgamesh:
"Truly, O Gilgamesh, one like thee
Has been born on the steppe,
Whom the open country has reared.
When thou seest him, thou wilt rejoice [as (over) a woman].
The heroes will kiss his feet;
Thou wilt embrace him. . . .
(And) wilt lead him to me."*

This dream clearly revolves about mother. It is related to her by Gilgamesh and she is the one who interprets the dream, saying that a collaborator or ally will join him—as if to replace mother, who has gone as far as she can with her son. The theme of the dream is the making of the hero and his reaching for the stars—for power—but the task is too heavy and too awesome for even a hero to handle alone; helpers are a necessity both for physical and moral support.

The second dream of Gilgamesh, also revolving about

* A. Heidel, *The Gilgamesh Epic and Old Testament Parallels,* University of Chicago Press.

mother, lays bare the symbolism of violent power inherent in the ax—a very special ax endowed with unusual potential. Gilgamesh again recounts to his mother:

> "[.......] in the street
> [Of Uru]k, the market place,
> There lay an ax,
> And they were gathered around it.
> As for the ax itself, its form was different (from
>   that of others).
> I looked at it and I rejoiced,
> Loving it and bending over it
> As (over) a woman.
> I took it and put it at my side."

Clearly, the link is made between the ax—or the use of violence, conquest—and the openly implied sexuality of bending over a woman.

Bertolt Brecht, a modern playwright, uses a similar metaphor in the mythical themes in his *Baal*. Brecht describes the omnipotent poet who desperately tries to be a man but who ruthlessly uses both men and women. He even murders his best friend and is in turn slain. To become a man, "you trample an enemy into the dust, you bend a woman's body over a bed."

As in the second dream of Gilgamesh, the striving for power becomes synonymous with the sexual triumph over a woman.

After Gilgamesh's first two dreams of daring ambition, he fells the mighty cedar tree (symbol of authority) and slays Humbaba, the terrible ogre who guards the sacred cedar forest. He then repels the advances of the love goddess Ishtar, being aware of her promiscuity and treachery. This rebuff infuriates Ishtar; she seeks permission from her father, the great god Anu, to have the Bull of Heaven slay Gilgamesh. Anu, in granting her request, reminds her that the slaying of a hero would cause a seven-year famine. Ishtar has anticipated this dire consequence and assures Anu that she has laid up a seven-year supply of food.

Then Came the Nightmares

In later dreams of Gilgamesh:

The mountains toppled, the heavens roared, the earth resounded, daylight failed, darkness came, lightning flashed, fire blazed, the clouds thickened, raining death,

. . . .

The brightness vanished, the fire went out;
and that which fell down turned to ashes.

Subsequently, Enkidu has a dream foreboding his own speedy end; the gods assemble to deliberate which of the two who killed Humbaba and the Bull of Heaven shall die. The lot falls on Enkidu, and he dies. Gilgamesh cries "bitterly like unto a wailing woman." For seven days and seven nights he weeps over his friend, hoping he will rise back to life. In the end, after failing at all attempts to seek immortality for himself, Gilgamesh reluctantly accepts the inevitability of death for all.

Dreams of Ancient Rome

The open incest dreams of the Roman leaders are treated in quite an acceptable manner by their dream seers. These dreams too are connected with ambition and with successful conquest.

Julius Caesar is reported to have had a dream of sexual intercourse with his mother. The dream interpreters of his day explained this as a favorable omen that he will take possession of the earth (mother earth).

The oracle given to the Tarquins prophesied that the conquest of Rome would fall to the one of them who should first kiss his mother.

Herodotus reports the dream of Hippias:

As for the Persians, they were guided to Marathon by Hippias. In the past night, he had seen a vision in his sleep wherein he thought that he lay with his mother; he interpreted this dream to signify that he would return to Athens and recover his power, and so die an old man in his own mother country.

Freud comments:

These myths and interpretations reveal a true psychological insight. I have found that people who know that they are preferred or loved by their mothers give evidence in their lives of a peculiar self-reliance and an unshakable optimism which often seem like heroic attributes and bring actual success to their possessors.

The Trouble with Being a Hero

Dreams of omnipotence too readily turn into nightmares. The hero of today becomes the victim of tomorrow; the mighty are too easily toppled by the jealous and the greedy, who are obsessed with their own inadequacies and lust for power. Flying dreams turn into the nightmarish terrors of falling. The blissful recurrent theme in both painting and dreams of Madonna and Child is balanced out by the equally recurrent theme of crucifixion. It is as if there were a harsh censor at work to make the punishment fit the crime for any sustained exhilaration from huge success or power.

Modern-Day Warriors and Heroes

In the summer of 1941, just a few days after the German invasion of Russia, Goebbels announced to the world, "We have smashed the Red Army to splinters. The Eastern continent lies like a limp virgin in the mighty arms of the German Mars."

Tolstoy, in his *War and Peace*, describes in painful detail the long, bloody Battle of Borodin. After the battle, Napoleon triumphantly views the cherished prize, Moscow.

Every Russian gazing at Moscow feels she is the mother; every foreigner gazing at her, and ignorant of her significance as the mother city, must be aware of the feminine character of the town, and Napoleon felt it.

A city occupied by the enemy is like a girl who has lost her honour. And from that point of view, he gazed at the oriental beauty who lay for the first time before his eyes.

As in *Gilgamesh,* there are seen to be direct links between seeking power, conquest by the hero, and the cherished goal of the fair maiden. What makes the pursuit of this conquest so enticing is that the prize is a virgin—untouched and unviolated by other men—the precise fantasy that a young boy has of his mother, and his keen desire to possess her and win her over. Needless to say, the whole business of conquest is a forbidden and most dangerous game.

A Twentieth-Century Odyssey

The warrior is not only the conqueror. The besieged and those seeking refuge can be warriors too. In some contemporary dreams from a child survivor of the holocaust in which his parents perished we see that he had been fighting enemies since he was two years old. He was later to become an Israeli soldier, but his whole life was a reliving of the dangers, flights, and aloneness of childhood, the constant battle for survival, and the yearning toward a maternal haven. The dreams:

"There are bombings of a railroad, fleeing, running, dogs chasing me, a concentration camp. I will be shot. I want only one thing—a glass of cold lemonade."

"I am defending a hill with other soldiers. The commander comes and tells me to pull back, to vacate the position. I refuse. I shoot him dead. Afterwards, in town, I see the same officer I shot dead. He is alive and says that he will report me. I say that I will deny the whole thing."

"I am swimming in the beautiful Sea of Galilee. There is a large swimming competition of many swimmers. On the shore there are grape vines, the roots of which turn into a snake. I wrestle with the snake and grab it by the neck."

"In technicolor, I dream of the beautiful fields, the flowers, the strawberries. Then I freeze in my tracks—watch out! In the bushes—it's El Fatah!"

"I am moved to tears by the sight of Jerusalem. I am riding on a train to visit my adopted parents."

In shooting his commanding officer, the dreamer feels a ruthless quality in himself—never to retreat or to give up, and to defy all authority. There appears to be a strong residue of guilt over his father's death—in some way he still feels responsible—the inevitable guilt of the survivor, which he is trying to overcome.

There is always danger, always competition, always a struggle for life and existence. The snake is the primordial symbol of treachery and death; in the dream he is also struggling with his own inner daemonic forces. He is able to accept his own need to survive successfully, which for him is like being a killer. Who can stand this killer! He would at times rather be alone, ostracized and unloved, than to get all that he wants. But it's kill or be killed.

The beauty of Jerusalem beckons and sustains; she may very well be a substitute for his dead mother—a highly coveted and prized possession of lovely bejeweled, gentle rolling hills. So many converging armies have been fighting over this prized city for almost three thousand years!

Knights of Old

A young man who has been drifting in and out of schools and jobs takes a big step by deciding to become a serious professional. For him this means competition and assuming the role of man-father, something which he has not dared until now. This triggers off the following dream:

"There are many knights, as of old, on horses, with pointed lances in a magnificent setting like Grand Canyon. There is a furious battle raging. A huge knight in armor confronts me. I am the youngest fighter. I am armed only with a small Swiss army knife. I find a rusted pitchfork and a bent sword and throw them at him. We roll on the ground locked in combat.

"The scene changes. We are sitting at a table in contemporary civilian clothes. I recognize him as my adversary before he sees me. He is still out to kill me if he recognizes me. I strike first. I take a sugar container, as thin as an eggshell, and hit him over the head with it and he falls dead. As a result of this action on my part, Israel will live as a nation; otherwise the State would have died. I am being pursued again; the battle goes on."

For this dreamer, life has been a bitter, dangerous struggle. To offset being the youngest, outfitted with inadequate weaponry, he gives himself omnipotent powers. He can kill a giant with an "eggshell," and in so doing he is the savior of his people and a nation. But what awesome power and responsibility to bear and such grave dangers for a boy to face all of his life. Little David slays the mighty Goliath!

A Medal of Honor Winner: A President Resigns

A professional man of thirty, riddled with excessive ambition, has driven himself much too hard. His grim and desperate pursuit of excellence and eminence has been his only method to make himself feel beyond reproach and to feel worthy. He has these dreams:

"I am a Vietnam hero, a Medal of Honor Winner. I won it for great feats and exploits; one of them was saving the lives of men and escaping through fifty miles of enemy territory."

"I am the President of the United States. I resign during my second term because there have been too many threats on my life."

The dreams symbolize the enormous unnecessary and dangerous tasks he has placed upon himself to be great and to exceed his elder brothers. Such excessive ambition can be most perilous, as, fortunately, the dreamer is beginning to realize. Like other "Presidents," he sees that the office of the chief executive has its many risks.

The dreams are clear warnings to let up and not push his luck and his drive too far. That he recognizes the dangers involved and is letting up on his ambitions is evidence that he is heeding the vital message of the dream.

Assassination and Aloneness

This dreamer is a professional man in his middle thirties who has always felt essentially alone, abandoned, and unappreciated. He now feels more ambition in his professional endeavors than ever, and also seeks to establish a better life. He has this series of dreams:

"I feel so alone, all alone."

"I want to go up in an elevator, but they are on strike."

"I am in some kind of collusion with President John Kennedy's wife to assassinate the President. I succeed in doing so by shooting him through a large glass window. I see the bullet pass through the window and then through his head. I am satisfied."

"There is a very distraught woman whom I comfort and give much time. I have to leave, but arrange to meet her later. When I return, she is not there. I am very disappointed and angry."

In the dreams is seen the connection between ambition, the recurrent fantasy of the boy violently wishing to replace the unsuspecting privileged father, and the queen mother who is a not-so-innocent bystander. But how can the fruits of such a foul deed be enjoyed? How can the plotting wife be trusted?

It is a hollow triumph for the victorious son; he dooms himself unnecessarily to eternal solitude—echoes of Hamlet's not being able to gain his desired throne. Like the tragic prince, he feels abandoned and betrayed by an ungrateful mother.

For this dreamer, ambition and success still have too many negative tie-ups with the original "primal sin" of wishing to get rid of father; hence, the sought-after prize of the woman remains elusive and excessive ambition is thwarted by distrust and guilt.

Kill or be killed is a common theme in dreams. Assassination—the killing off of a mighty leader—is a form of patricide. It is gambling for the highest stakes possible— full power, or death as the penalty for such a violent transgression.

Such an assassination dream is fully enacted in the actual murder of a president by a demented mind who knows no limits or controls over wild dreams of power, insane jealousy, and stark hatred. The mind of the despot dictator likewise knows no division or restraint between the original dream or fantasy and the ruthless mass murder that is thought necessary to fulfill the wish for ultimate total power. Plato said, "The innocent man dreams of what the scoundrel does."

Such dreams of ambition and violence are not to be feared; they reflect the natural fantasies of any bright, active boy who wishes to be a king with power of life and death over others. Reliving these old fantasies in adult dreams is a healthy way of facing and accepting the worst "crimes" of the past, so as not to feel forever ruthless and hunted.

Let the Sleeping Warrior Lie . . . to Dream

It is better to dream than to fight! Men need no longer have to be the perpetual duelers of old, ever conquering new worlds and defending themselves against all the threatening forces of the world.

In their dreams, men can face and overcome the terrors of the past so as not to inflict them needlessly upon themselves or other men. Each man need not be the pursued victim forever, and may instead find satisfaction and trust with those close. Dreams of violence need not be enacted.

Dreams can be tamed, provided we are free enough to see and understand them. Violent dreams can become less intense and less frequent. The occasional nightmare that does occur can be handled and understood so that we come through with a good sense of ourselves.

Our Links with the Past

It is never easy to grow up, especially if one nurtures the ambitions of a favored son sparked by an ambitious mother. To mature, the hero must simultaneously maintain and sever close ties with mother and constantly resort to fighting the forces that would annihilate him.

The ancient dreams of the *Gilgamesh* epic show how little human beings have changed in the past four thousand years. The basic themes of the story—the struggle of the hero to achieve power, defy authority, face the continuous dangers of sex and death, and to seek immortality—have accompanied all mankind and his dreams ever since. There are always the nightmares of the coming cataclysm—the destruction of the world for daring to challenge the powers of the gods.

The fascination of dreams is that despite their uniqueness—each dream is different from every other dream that has ever been created—they all spring from certain basic themes which stretch across all peoples, all cultures, and all ages. When we understand one dream—any dream—we, in turn, better understand both ourselves and all humanity with its long history of eternal dishonor and triumph. The dream is a kind of cultural link to the past; it is our common history of emotional experiences. The dream rings unconscious bells and filters through to give us better awareness of what people are.

X

Biblical Dreams

Interestingly enough, the first dream in Genesis revolves about power and lust in no less a personage than King Abimelech. The king becomes involved with Abraham and Sarah, who are passing through his kingdom of Gerar. The king is attracted to Sarah and takes her to his palace, not knowing that she is married. Abraham, fearing for his life, has told the king that Sarah is his sister (which is true; she is his half-sister).

But God came to Abimelech in a dream by night, and said to him, Behold, thou art but a dead man, for the woman which thou hast taken; for she is a man's wife.

But Abimelech had not come near her: and he said, Lord, wilt thou slay also a righteous nation?

Said he not unto me, She is my sister? And she, even she herself said, He is my brother: in the integrity of my heart and innocency of my hands have I done this.

And God said unto him in a dream, Yea. I know that thou didst this in the integrity of thy heart; for I also withheld thee from sinning against me: therefore suffered I thee not to touch her.

Now therefore restore the man his wife; for he is a prophet, and he shall pray for thee, and thou shalt live: and if thou restore her not, know thou that thou shalt surely die, thou, and all that are thine.

The lesson to draw is clear. Even a king cannot covet another man's wife; when he does so, he jeopardizes not only his own life but the lives of all the people of the kingdom. However, even the strict teachings and prohibitions of the early testament are inconsistent and contradictory. In the story of King David, the young king does something far more terrible than the duped Abimelech. David not only knowingly lies with Uriah's wife, but impregnates her and then treacherously arranges Uriah's death in battle. David is then free to marry Bathsheba. An angered God does not slay David or his people, but nonetheless does punish him severely by causing his new son to die. This recurrent problem in the Bible underscores powerful temptations of the Forbidden Flesh besetting all mortals, and the inevitable threat of retribution—even for kings.

Jacob's Ladder Dream

The second dream in Genesis also has to do with ambition, even while the dreamer is sleeping on a lowly hard stone:

And he dreamed, and behold a ladder set up on the earth, and the top of it reached to heaven; and behold, the angels of God ascending and descending on it.

It must be remembered that Jacob is the favorite son of his mother, Rebecca. It is Rebecca who engineers the deception against her eldest son, Esau, whereby Jacob appears before his blind father, Isaac, for the important blessing of the eldest son. According to Hebraic custom, on the death of the father the eldest son received a double share of the inheritance and became head of the family. When Esau learns of his brother's deception, he is out for blood, and Jacob must flee for his life, just as later Joseph has cause to fear for his life at the hands of his irate brothers. From Jacob's ladder dream, it is evident that he, as the new leader of his people, is very, very special, not only in the eyes of his mother but also by virtue of having direct and continuous access to the holiest source of power.

Again, the lonely mortal dares to take on godly powers. But it is a dangerous game, and his very life is jeopardized. The hero's mother, as in the *Gilgamesh* epic, is always on the scene, behind the scene, and in the dream. A ladder is like a bridge or an indestructible link between mother and son and the very special ambitions which a mother invokes in her favorite son.

Jacob becomes the Biblical prototype of the leader who feels he has special powers and special missions to perform. This is a story which shows the make-up of a leader of a people and how he succeeds in making his dream of omnipotence come true for the good of his tribe.

The Joseph Dreams

The Genesis story of Joseph and his brothers and its direct mythological antecedents are possibly five thousand years old. This saga of intrigue and moral triumph is one of the most universally appealing stories and to this day is a favorite of all ages. Here is a recounting which is both naïvely simple and unfathomably complex, with its wide gamut of action and feeling, encompassing powerful life motifs interwoven with ambition, hatred, jealousy, lust, and fear. The resolution evolved, however, consists of Joseph's decision to do what is best for his people, while simultaneously satisfying his own omnipotent strivings.

There appears in the Joseph story a total of six dreams. All of the other dreams presented in the Old Testament are single or isolated; however, concentrated in this relatively brief narrative are two dreams of Joseph while he is still living with his family. Later came the dream of the deposed chief butler and the unfortunate dream of the doomed chief baker. These are followed by the most famous dreams of all literature: the two dreams of Pharaoh, which Joseph so nimbly and accurately utilizes in his successful prophecies.

We shall examine in these dreams the diverse aspects and stages of development of the drives and conflicts of the religious leader as personified by Joseph.

Joseph is to his mother, Rachel, an even more special son than his father, Jacob, has been to Rebecca. Joseph is his mother's only son until her untimely death in giving birth to Benjamin. Rachel is Jacob's true love; he far prefers her to her older sister, Leah, whom he was tricked into marrying. Jacob has had six sons with Leah; four more sons have been conceived with the handmaidens Bilah and Zilpah. Rachel gives birth to Joseph only after years of barrenness. She finally conceives, with Leah's

connivance, after her youngest son, Reuben, finds the
mandrake with its magical power of fertility; the son is
therefore seen to have played an indirect role in concep-
tion. There can be no doubt that a first son born to Rachel
under such trying circumstances would have to be the
highly treasured and indulged favorite of his mother.
Joseph is also his father's favorite; Jacob identifies completely with him and feels that he is the fairest, and
probably the most intelligent, of all his twelve sons.
Joseph must know this, for how else are we to account for
the two dreams when he is seventeen years of age? Note,
too, the aroused ire of the brothers and of even Jacob:

And Joseph dreamed a dream, and he told it to his brethren:
and they hated him yet the more. . . .
For, behold, we were binding sheaves in the field, and, lo,
my sheaf arose, and also stood upright; and, behold, your
sheaves stood round about and made obeisance to my sheaf.
And his brethren said to him, shalt thou indeed reign over
us? or shalt thou indeed have dominion over us? And they
hated him yet the more for his dreams, and for his words.
And he dreamed yet another dream, and told it to his
brethren, and said, Behold, I have dreamed a dream more; and,
behold, the sun and the moon and the eleven stars made obeisance to me.
And he told it to his father, and to his brethren: and his
father rebuked him, and said unto him, What is this dream that
thou hast dreamed. Shall I and thy mother and thy brethren
indeed come to bow down ourselves to thee to the earth?

The exaggerated and omnipotent meanings of the
dream are compounded by the repetition of the same
theme, the second dream being even more pronounced

and grandiose than the first. The first dream is a more earthly and provincial undertaking and may relate to the earliest fantasies of the young boy becoming proudly aware of his masculine attributes and their prerogatives. The second dream certainly embraces the cosmos and is an extension and mushrooming of the first dream into the very heavens. It encompasses not only the earth but the entire universe as well, so that Joseph becomes a true godly figure. What greater power could there be than to be bowed to by the sun, the moon, and the stars—to become the very center of the universe about which all revolves?

The use to which Joseph puts these dreams is in this instance more important than the dreams themselves. To boast arrogantly to his brothers of dreams with such obvious meanings is either to be naïve in the extreme or to invite a most certain retaliatory display of hatred, which Joseph must feel to be necessary and deserved. For his own safety he needs to have his fantasies and mounting ambitions curbed before he is destroyed by his aroused, jealous brothers, who must have regarded him as a young interloper threatening their powers and rights.

After Joseph's arrogantly taunting dreams, his brothers seek bloody vengeance, but because of Reuben's intervention our dreamer is instead cast into a pit. Judah then talks his brothers into selling Joseph to some Ishmaelites on their way to Egypt rather than killing him.

In Egypt Joseph is sold by some Midianites to Potiphar, an officer of the Pharaoh and Captain of the Guard. Joseph impresses his master and is made overseer of the household. Ultimately, Joseph impresses his master's wife,

Zuleika, as well, and she propositions him to lie with her.

Fear and panic cause Joseph to flee from his master's wife. Unfortunately, however, so great is his haste that he neglectfully leaves his garment in Zuleika's hand; this is his undoing. Once again in literature the reticent lover is framed by the scorned woman, and, her wrath knowing no bounds, she lands him in jail. Joseph's chastity is of no avail after all.

It is in prison, however, that Joseph has the first opportunity to demonstrate his undeniable talent as an interpreter of dreams.

Pharaoh's chief butler and baker have both fallen into disfavor. Both of them dream their dreams in the same night.

A Butler and a Baker Dream

The butler:

> In my dream, behold, a vine was before me;
> And in the vine were three branches: . . . and her blossoms shot forth; and the clusters thereof brought forth ripe grapes:
> And Pharaoh's cup was in my hand: and I took the grapes, and pressed them into Pharaoh's cup, and I gave the cup into Pharaoh's hand.
> And Joseph said unto him, This is the interpretation of it: The three branches are three days:
> Yet within three days shall Pharaoh lift up thine head, and restore thee unto thy place: and thou shalt deliver Pharaoh's cup into his hand, after the former manner when thou wast his butler.

The baker:

When the chief baker saw that the interpretation was good, he said unto Joseph, I also was in my dream, and, behold, I had three white baskets on my head:

And in the uppermost basket there was all manner of bake-meats for Pharaoh; and the birds did eat them out of the basket upon my head.

And Joseph answered and said, This is the interpretation thereof: The three baskets are three days:

Yet within three days shall Pharaoh lift up thy head from off thee, and shall hang thee on a tree; and the birds shall eat thy flesh from off thee.

While the dreams of Joseph may be considered as the prevailing wishes of the omnipotent child, the dreams of the chief butler and baker may be regarded as linked to the adolescent crisis of transition into early adulthood. These are powerful and dangerous dreams, for upon them hinge life itself; they portend the actual confrontation between life and death for the dreamers. These dreams represent the polarities of male adjustment in terms of either discreet obeisance to the authority of the ruler, or the opposite, the uncontrolled fulfillment of primary passions and ambitions which can ultimately be death-dealing if unleashed indiscriminately.

In the bird symbolism of the chief baker's dream, such associations as deity, death, and dangerous-forbidden-sexuality-unleashed have been made. From earliest times God has been symbolically depicted at one time or another as a powerful bird descending from the heavens and endowed with stern, vindictive, and magical powers. The bird-gods of the Egyptian kingdom of death were also associated with the world of hell; this concept symbolizes the first antithesis between the higher world of religion and the lower world of sex, between heaven and hell.

There is in the butler's dream the expected degree of control and submission to authority necessary to weather the adolescent crisis. The ripening virility, so potentially dangerous, is safely diverted. The alternative is the fate of the baker; here the bird of reckless youth gets out of hand and dares to eat of the forbidden fruit meant for the exclusive consumption of the mighty Pharaoh. Such audacity could not go unpunished, and so the sweet bird of youth becomes the tragic forebear of death.

Joseph's prophecies of these two dreams prove accurate and are instrumental in eventually freeing him from prison. He must then face the supreme test of interpreting Pharaoh's dreams, which up to then have defied the efforts of all the dream seers of the land.

The Pharaoh's Dreams

The Pharaoh's two dreams, occurring on the same night, are most difficult to fathom, and are most likely the real key to the understanding of the total dream series. Joseph interprets these dreams when he is thirty years old.

And it came to pass at the end of two full years, that Pharaoh dreamed: and, behold, he stood by the river.

And, behold, there came up out of the river seven well favored kine and fat-fleshed; and they fed in a meadow.

And, behold, seven other kine came up after them out of the river, ill-favored and lean-fleshed; and stood by the other kine upon the brink of the river.

And the ill-favored and lean-fleshed kine did eat up the seven well-favored and fat kine. So Pharaoh awoke.

And he slept and dreamed the second time: and, behold, seven ears of corn came up upon one stalk, rank and good.

And, behold, seven thin ears and blasted with the east wind sprung up after them.

And the seven thin ears devoured the seven rank and full ears. And Pharaoh awoke, and, behold, it was a dream.

And Joseph said unto Pharaoh, The dream of Pharaoh is one: God hath showed Pharaoh what he is about to do.

The seven good kine are seven years; and the seven good ears are seven years: the dream is one.

And the seven thin and ill-favored kine that came up after them are seven years; and the seven empty ears blasted with the east wind shall be seven years of famine.

It is not accidental that *cow* and *corn* are used as the two principal symbolic elements of Pharaoh's dreams; both are life-giving, lifting man from the precarious nomad existence of the hunter. Both cattle and corn represent a constant, seemingly never-ending supply of essential nourishment for full security and satiety. This is in keeping with the figure seven, which enters so prominently in the dreams, for the Hebrew word for seven is *shevah,* meaning satiety or plenty. The Hebrew word for corn is *shivalim,* which translated means stream or current; again a constant supply or never-ending gush.

The prosperity of ancient Egypt was contingent upon the annual inundation by the Nile. In the Egyptian legend "The Tradition of Seven Lean Years in Egypt," the origin of the Nile is described. In the legend there is a city in the midst of the waters from which the Nile rises, called Elephantine (the mound on which creation took place); within are two underground caverns which are considered the two true breasts that pour forth all good things.

With the seven lean years in Egypt, the flow stops and the fertility of the land and the growth of corn ceases. The "seven" stands for the polar extremes of satiety or starvation—perhaps the two faces of mother who gives all or too much and then another time withholds all in anger.

The figure "seven" is prominent too in early creation myths. In Judaism "seven" is also connected with death and immortality. There are seven days of mourning for the dead. During these days the soul of the departed one is still tied to the earth; after that time it returns to its creator.

In ancient Egyptian civilization the gods were associated with and represented by animals. The figure of the mother goddess was especially prominent and was known in the form of a cow as Hathor. Hathor was the principle of love and fertility; she was also revered as a moon goddess and as the deity who received the dead in the other world, offering the promise of immortality or life after death shared with mother.

The Mystery of Corn

Pharaoh is especially troubled by the second of his two dreams. It does not make sense that ears of corn could be swallowed up by other ears of corn.

This animal function applied to corn is not so mysterious when we consider the sacred importance with which corn was regarded and its intimate connection with life and death, fertility and resurrection. Corn was the symbol of eternity of life, and its annual harvest symbolized the death of divine life. Corn was what sustained life and it was considered miraculously sent by gods to save the people of Egypt in time of famine.

For the Egyptians, the personified chief of corn, or corn god, was identified with Osiris, the god of nature and fertility, who was treacherously murdered by his brother Set. In the temple of Isis the dead body of Osiris was represented with stalks of corn springing from it. Osiris was eventually dismembered by his infuriated brother, cut into many pieces, and scattered throughout the land, symbolizing the sowing of the corn.

In many myths corn is seen as symbolic of something less than idyllic. Here is the competitive struggle to the death of the brothers and the final resurrection of the slain combatant through the growth of corn. The clash between Joseph and his brothers never reaches such a state of primitive brutality and represents a most refined advancement in the classic struggle of brothers. Instead of being slain and buried, or planted in the ground like the harvested corn, Joseph is merely cast awhile into the pit, from which he eventually comes forth to be the savior in producing the life-saving corn.

Being Eaten Up

Being eaten up is the predominant theme of Pharaoh's dreams; it is linked with the struggle for power within the tribe.

The fear of being eaten or swallowed is freely verbalized by anxious young children, and it figures prominently in childhood nightmares. In these dreams, as well as in many fairy tales, the devouring host is usually some form of large animal, witch, or giant.

When Joseph's brothers first conspire against him, they plan to slay him and cast him into some pit, "and we will say, Some evil beast hath devoured him." Later they recant, kill a kid goat instead, dip Joseph's coat of many colors into the blood, and show the stained garment to their father, Jacob. The aggrieved father exclaims, "It is my son's coat; an evil beast hath devoured him."

Pharaoh's dreams are the most disguised and symbolic of all the dreams in the Joseph story. It is felt that they represent the most primitive or latent hidden wishes and fears confronting any leader, not only Pharaoh; hence the dreams pertain to Joseph's earliest fantasy life as well. In the Biblical story these dreams provide a vehicle more for Joseph than for Pharaoh. Joseph is thereby able to rise above his earliest omnipotent ambitions—originally self-serving, but also self-destructive. Joseph has been compared to Napoleon in terms of their unique closeness with their mothers and their similar ambitions to be great saviors and to show up their brothers. But what a difference in accomplishments! What diverse alternatives are there that face leaders, as they relate to childhood dilemmas. One path leads to senseless, insatiable, bloody conquest in which millions of lives are sacrificed or made miserable; the other path leads to peace and plenty for all, in spite of real famine. Unlike Napoleon, Joseph overcomes many internal barriers, as is shown in the dream series, and in the end is able to enjoy love, sex, and power all at once. His dreams and his ability to handle them perhaps did the trick.

In the Joseph story, through the six dreams in the series studied along with related mythology, may be seen the evolution of the benevolent leader. Here emerges a power that is exercised with full wisdom and tact in comparison to the self-destructive conceit and brashness of his adolescent dreams.

Joseph becomes a symbol of the link between the small clan of early Israelites and the outside world. He breaks through to the larger community and makes his indelible mark by contributing his unique genius to his host. Joseph is able to rise above his own ambitions and desire in utilizing his talents for the good of a nation and for his own people. He not only is able to rise above the common foibles of his contemporaries, but as the leader, he does not, out of fear or guilt or corrupting inner weakness, have to either punish himself further or tempt ultimate destruction by seeking further power or display prowess through battle.

In Genesis we have seen the prototypes of the earliest leaders of an emerging primitive people, initially no less savage than any of the other numerous nomadic tribes which converged on the land of Canaan. The book of Genesis ends with the Joseph story and the taming and channeling of ambition, pride, distrust, and hateful vengeance—any of which is enough to destroy any person or people.

In the examples of Esau, Reuben, Judah, and Joseph, the primitive law of talion underwent its first radical change. In their reaction to follow the natural inclination for revenge, the brothers all forgave one another eventually and lived together in peace. The violence of Genesis reached its height in the barbaric castration and slaying of the tribe of Shechem by Joseph's brothers, led by Simeon and Levi. This brutal period of the earliest Jews was symbolically resolved by the Joseph story to set an example for all men and all leaders.

It is men like the prophets of the Bible, with their many prophetic visions and dreams, whose unenviable job it is to expose injustice, to rebuke, to warn, to cajole, to rage, and to threaten, lest moral corruption get too much out of hand and destroy all. The prophets feel and fight fiercely, shun popularity, care not to please; they disquiet complacency; they are considered troublemakers by the entrenched and conforming. Their dreams shake and even topple kingdoms.

Present-Day Messages from the Joseph Story

Dreams and Bible stories do not deal with storytelling only; they handle crucial issues dealing with physical and moral survival for the individual, the family, and whole peoples. In the dreams of the Joseph story, first you see natural ambition, rivalry, and jealousy of the brothers reaching ugly proportions of hatred and near violence. This is no different from the feelings that exist in most families, though they are usually covered up. It is not so terrible when siblings battle as long as blood is not shed, and in the end they learn to appreciate and help each other.

It is also inevitable that certain children are favored, but parents should be aware of the detrimental effect this can have, not only on the other children but on the favored child as well. Of course, this special child may thereby develop the competent self-reliance of the future benevolent leader, but he or she can also turn out to be a tyrant.

The dreams of the baker and butler and the sexual temptations confronting Joseph give us understanding into the difficult alternatives confronting youth in their intense conflict of ambition and passion.

Pharaoh's dreams demonstrate for us the alternatives facing leaders and parents alike—to live peacefully with proper planning, cooperative effort, and regard for everyone, or to encourage clannishness, jealousy, distrust, and greed.

XI

Can Dreams Predict Events?

The power of dreams to foretell the future offers endless intriguing possibilities. Freud himself felt that while there is no question that dreams give us knowledge of the future, it would be truer to say instead that they give us knowledge of the past: "For dreams are derived from the past in every sense. . . . By picturing our wishes fulfilled, dreams are after all leading us into the future. But this future, which the dreamer pictures as the present, has been moulded by his indestructible wish into a perfect likeness of the past."

However, some of the dreams that follow raise questions and possibilities which cannot be ignored. In time of war especially there are many dreams of loved ones being dead, wounded, or captured. How many of these dreams are accurate in their prophecy is impossible to know. We hear only of those dreams that prove accurate. In times of stress, dreaming is rampant—wishing for the best, and expecting and preparing for the worst. The unbearable mounting tension and anxiety know their only nocturnal relief in the dream and thereby help to preserve a measure of sanity.

Dreams of people dying (except perhaps under real conditions of tragedy and danger) usually have nothing to do with death, but rather the opposite. It is the fear of full living or full sexuality which triggers off exaggerated anticipations of the worst dreaded happenings and related punishment.

Dreams of dying or of loved ones dying by no means imply that these are necessarily our wishes or that these sad events are likely to transpire. These dreams may also reflect a new appreciation of life and people, before it is too late.

Winston Churchill Dreams of Dying

Winston Churchill, the day before the election which he lost to the Labor party in 1945, had an unpleasant dream:

I dreamed that life was over. I saw—it was very vivid—my dead body under a white sheet. . . . I thought: perhaps this is the end.

His greatest accomplishments were behind him, even though he went on to live for twenty years after the dream. As a shrewd, seasoned politician, however, he must have sensed political defeat, which for a man in his position, as a highly effective Prime Minister during all the many difficult war years of England's greatest peril, must have been particularly humiliating and bitter.

A Warning of an Assassination . . . Unheeded

Abraham Lincoln had a premonitory dream of his death a few days before his assassination. At that time he remarked that he had been greatly impressed by the number of dream prophecies and warnings in the Bible. "If we believe the Bible we must accept the fact that in the old days God and his angels came to men in their sleep and made themselves known in dreams. Nowadays dreams are regarded as very foolish, and are seldom told, except by old women and young men and maidens in love."

Mrs. Lincoln asked why he had raised the subject, and Lincoln then described a dream in which, wandering through the White House, he saw a coffin guarded by soldiers, and a throng of weeping people. "Who is dead?" he asked in the dream. The answer was: "The president, killed by an assassin."

Lincoln, in his brooding ways, must have felt the heavy guilt of the enormous bloodshed of the Civil War. He could not have been unmindful of the many people who blamed him for the conduct of the war and who hated him bitterly; yet he took no extra precautions for his own safety after his harrowing nightmare.

Oil in the Desert Revealed in a Dream

In 1937 an English gentleman, Lieutenant Colonel H. R. P. Dickson, the British political agent and real ruler of Kuwait, dreamed a dream:

One day, a violent sandstorm carved a hole by a palm tree in his compound, and that night he dreamed that he approached the hole and found a sarcophagus. Upon touching the shroud within, a beautiful maiden rose to life. Then he heard the shouts of some strangers in the desert who seized the sobbing girl and tried to bury her alive. Colonel Dickson chased the men away, then woke up.

Perplexed by his vision, he consulted a Bedouin woman renowned for her power of prophecy, who told him that the girl in the sarcophagus was the harbinger of riches beneath the sand of Kuwait and that the men were strangers from across the sea who wished to prevent its discovery. The Colonel should go to the diggers at Bahrah, tell them to abandon that place and proceed instead to the desert of Burgan. There, by a lonely palm tree, they would find a great treasure.

For two years, a British team had been drilling dry wells at Bahrah on Kuwait Bay, but they laughed at Colonel Dickson when he told them of his dream and urged them to try Burgan, about 30 miles south. Undaunted, he sailed to London and recounted his dream to the company executives. One of them, a believer in dreams and prophecies, cabled Kuwait and transferred the team to Burgan. There, in May of 1938, by a lonely palm tree, they struck oil.*

It is difficult to resist the power of the dream and the mysticism of the soothsayer's highly adept interpretations. The fascinating aspect of the dream is that the beautiful maiden symbolizes the inaccessible treasure of the oil, so hard to reach, to touch. It is like a modern-day fairy tale of a sleeping beauty, a dormant treasure discovered and

* E. R. F. Sheehan, *New York Times Magazine*, March 24, 1974.

awakened by a handsome rescuer. Once again, the seizing of power and wealth becomes synonymous with the prized, elusive fair maiden.

A Soldier Dreams of Capture Before a War

An Israeli soldier who was taken prisoner in the Yom Kippur War has this dream account of the war to report:

"Two weeks before the outbreak of the war, my brigade was called up for routine reserve duty and sent to the Suez Canal opposite the Firdan bridge, north of Ismailia.

"As we stepped off the bus at the bridge, I was filled with misgivings. Just over two weeks before I was called up, I had dreamed a dream, the details of which I wrote down upon awakening. I dreamed of captivity in a strange land . . . myself a fugitive . . . and a gigantic bridge— the bridge at Firdan."

An Oriental Rug at Macy's

A young lady had a dream which she made sure came true:

"I dreamt that I was wandering alone in the Oriental rug department at Macy's department store. I admired all the fascinating beautiful colors and designs of the rugs, but I had no money. A fine-looking elderly gentleman noticed me and asked if I would like a rug. I picked out a nice small one. He bought it for me."

Of course, the next day she couldn't wait to get to Macy's rug department, and—wouldn't you know—there actually was a gallant man there who eventually noticed the plight of the fair damsel in obvious distress and actually fulfilled her dream. But such is the stuff out of which fairy tales are made.

So if one asks, "Are dreams prophetic?" the answer is that they can be. If you desire something so badly and will it so strongly, you can make the dream come true—of course, not beyond fairly reasonable limits. But then, who is to say what are reasonable limits?

XII.

How to Remember Dreams

If you are intent on remembering dreams and daring enough to leap into the unknown of another world, the dreams will come through. This is no mystery; we now know that every person dreams on the average of close to two hours a night, sometimes even more. Most people, however, choose not to remember their dreams, probably to avoid the feared repetition of early terrifying childhood nightmares. As adults, however, we can take the bad dreams along with the good. Dreaming is as natural and necessary as eating—a way of feeding ourselves, mostly in the early hours of morning when sleep is lightest.

If we are stimulated and motivated to remember our dreams and are not afraid of them, then we will grasp or latch on to any vivid key feeling, action, word, or person in the dream, which upon gradual awakening will usually trigger off the rest of the dream. Dreams can fade away fast, so at times you really have to concentrate to hold on to any lingering remnants; but if you lose them, don't worry. The dream will come back again in some form when your frame of mind is more receptive to grabbing the elusive vision. Some people immediately have to write down their dreams, but this is usually not essential.

If we connect the dream to the day's happenings preceding the dream, its meaning or message will fall into place more readily and help us understand or resolve future action.

All dreams, to some extent, spill out into the next day's moods or actions and influence them. Thus we should try to know as much as possible of what is going on so that we can better shape the course of our feelings and actions. We are then in a position to use some of the "magic" of the dream to work for us, instead of feeling like the child or primitive, at the mercy of the frightening grip of night terrors.

Hopefully, the reading of this book will help each person understand and reconcile to his or her own inner wild world of fantasy, to appreciate the many mysteries of the powerful feelings that inhabit the mind, and so be better able to accept, utilize, and enjoy his inner desires and thrusts. The main thing is to know and to feel rather than to fear, run, or hide.

Dreams and Life

~~~~~~

It is when dreams are linked up with the ideas and ideals of peoples that the dreams breathe true life and enduring spirit. Perhaps this is why the dreams of the Bible—especially the dreams in the Joseph story—are so powerful, deep, and enduring: they are concerned with the betterment of peoples, with leaders facing their own ambitions, fears, and self-destructiveness, so that they do not have to impose them upon the innocent multitudes. Man may be best meant to serve and still enjoy his full measure of life's pleasures.

Each man should have his own hill or mountain to climb, but each is of a different height; the rate of ascent should be geared to the emotional and physical capabilities of an individual, without the stumbling blocks of undue pressure to trip over up the paths. A well-tempered climb brings exhilaration and keen satisfaction without forced efforts, exhaustion, and resentment.

Dreaming is the spice and elixir of life; it can be the Fountain of Youth, the source and spring and preserver of life. The dream is nocturnal drama and song which shows us the way, sustains, inspires, and arouses all sorts of desire.

Even as nightmare the dream warns, protects, and strengthens. When inner conflicts become unbearable, when outer pressures are excessive, we seek the solace of our dreams to guide toward a future of greater pleasure, satisfaction, and safety.

There is really not that much to be afraid of if we know what we want, if we but listen to our dreams, understand them, and appreciate them as something very precious, which we ourselves provide daily, endlessly. Full dreaming is the necessary prelude to full living. The magic and the mysteries of dreams know no end.